T0169058

CULTURE SMART!

SAUDI
ARABIA

THE ESSENTIAL GUIDE TO
CUSTOMS & CULTURE

CHERYL OBAL

KUPERARD

"The real voyage of discovery consists not in seeking new landscapes, but in having new eyes."

Adapted from Marcel Proust, *Remembrance of Things Past*.

ISBN 978 1 78702 354 3

British Library Cataloguing in Publication Data
A CIP catalogue entry for this book is available
from the British Library

First published in Great Britain
by Kuperard, an imprint of Bravo Ltd
59 Hutton Grove, London N12 8DS
Tel: +44 (0) 20 8446 2440
www.culturesmart.co.uk
Inquiries: publicity@kuperard.co.uk

Design Bobby Birchall
Printed in Turkey

The Culture Smart! series is continuing to expand.
All Culture Smart! guides are available as e-books, and many
as audio books. For further information and latest titles visit
www.culturesmart.co.uk

CHERYL OBAL grew up in Pennsylvania, United States and has a Master's degree in International Relations from the University of Trieste, Italy. For the last twenty-five years she has lived and worked in numerous countries around the world, most often as a corporate trainer for multinational companies, including in Japan, South Korea, Thailand, India, Pakistan, and Saudi Arabia, where she has worked for more than eight years.

Today Cheryl is based in Vicenza, Italy, where she runs her own company offering cross-cultural training and consultation to companies and individuals from around the world. More about her work as a cross-cultural trainer can be found at cherylobal.com.

Aside from her intercultural work, Cheryl is also a professional choreographer and enjoys writing articles for her blog, reading, spending time with friends, and making videos for her YouTube channel about expat life and communicating across cultural divides.

CONTENTS

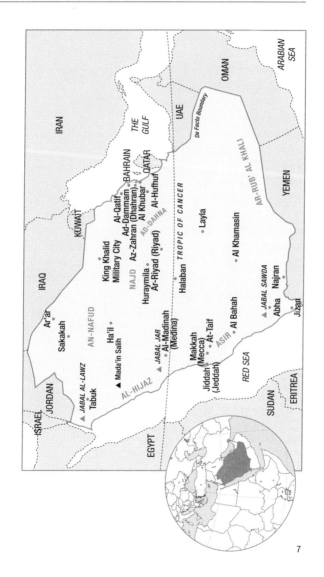

The Saudi Arabia of today is nothing like the Saudi Arabia of twenty years ago, or even ten years ago. In the past, the Arab Gulf nation was a closed, secretive country, a conservative Islamic society strictly guarded by Sharia law and closed to visitors except those coming for religious pilgrimage or work.

Now, the country is going through an extraordinary transformation that began in 2016 at the launch of Vision 2030, the plan that Saudi's leaders King Salman and Crown Prince Mohammed Bin Salman have devised to catapult the country into the future. More than an economic initiative that seeks to diversify the economy away from a dependence on oil revenues, it is a comprehensive plan that is driving forward changes on all aspects of life in the Kingdom. Whereas in the past, for example, there were few places people could gather in public, now there are open-air concerts, movie theaters, sports competitions, and industry conventions. Saudi Arabia's standard of living is receiving a serious upgrade: housing, healthcare, education, transportation, energy, and tourism (including now, for the first time, foreign tourism!) are all experiencing great development as part of the revolutionary initiatives. The rights of women and their position in Saudi society, too, is evolving.

The pace of change and its wider effects, particularly on Saudi society, cannot be understated. No matter who you talk to, from young Saudis to their parents, from businesspeople to housewives, practically everyone's face lights up with excitement when you discuss the topic with them—and the buzz is infectious. One reason for the optimism may well be because the key message that underlies the Vision is that the country's most valuable resource is not its oil, but rather its people. And it's the people that this book will introduce you to.

Currently, sixty-three percent of the Kingdom's population are under the age of thirty, a fact that bodes very well for the country's future. But while the population may be young, its culture is anything but. Human history in the region dates back millennia, and the Islamic civilization that emerged from the heartlands of Arabia in the seventh century has changed the world.

Some fourteen hundred years later, it is the values and principles of Islam that are sacred and form the foundations of Saudi culture. These include faith and worship of a single God, charity, the importance of community, and the observance of religious duties such as Hajj, the pilgrimage to Mecca that all Muslims are required to make at least once in their lives. Then, there are the values and ways of doing things that reflect Saudi Arabia's roots as a tribal society. These include values such as honor, hospitality, and loyalty to one's family and tribe. While tribal affiliations have become less prominent in modern Saudi as the country's national and civic identity has taken precedence, understanding its influence is important if one is to understand the full complexity of their Saudi hosts. All this and much more is unpacked in these pages. Those who take the time to learn about Saudi history, its culture, traditions, and way of life, will find that their experience in this unique country will be greatly enriched.

Official Name	Kingdom of Saudi Arabia (Al-Mamlaka al-Arabiya as-Saudiya)	Member of Arab League and Gulf Cooperation Council
Capital City	Riyadh	
Main Cities	Jeddah, Dammam, al-Khobar	
Population	Approx. 37,000,000, of whom 13.4 m are foreigners (2024)	Annual population growth rate 2.52%
Demography	Saudi 58.4%, Expat 41.6%	
Age Structure	0–14 years: 26% 15–64 years: 71% 65 years and over: 3%	
Area	864,869 square miles (2,240,000 sq. km)	
Geography	Middle East, bordering the Persian Gulf and the Red Sea, north of Yemen	Four regions: Hijaz, Najd, Eastern Province, South
Terrain	Mostly sandy desert. Rugged mountains along the west coast give way to a central plateau; the east is rocky or sandy lowland. The huge sandy desert to the south is hostile to life.	
Climate	Desert climate, with hot days and cold nights; hot and humid on the coast	
Natural Resources	Petroleum, natural gas, iron ore, gold, copper	
Currency	Saudi riyal (SAR) US $1 = SAR 3.75	

Language	Arabic	English is widely spoken, particularly by those under the age of forty.
Religion	Sunni Islam, Wahhabi	The religious establishment, the *ulema*, is headed by the Grand Mufti.
Minority Faiths	Shia Islam; Christianity, Hinduism, and other religions among expatriates	Islam remains the only official religion.
Government	Absolute monarchy	The king is head of state and cabinet; an appointed *shura* council advises; partial local elections
Media	Government controlled; satellite and streaming access to pan-Arab and international channels	Newspapers include *Al Jazeera*, *Okaz*, and *Al-Watan* (in Arabic); *Arab News* and *Saudi Gazette* (in English)
Electricity	230 volts, 60 Hz	Two- or three-prong plugs, depending on age of building
Internet Domain	.sa	Fiber optic broadband and 5G network conenctivity now covers most populated areas.
Telephone	The country code is 966.	To call abroad, dial 00 followed by country code
Time Zone	GMT + 3 hours	

CHAPTER ONE

LAND & PEOPLE

GEOGRAPHY

Saudi Arabia is a desert country about one-fifth the size of the United States, covering some 864,869 square miles (2,240,000 sq. km) of overwhelmingly arid land. While the landscape can look much the same across the Kingdom, the features that stand out do so spectacularly.

Only about 37 miles (60 km) south of the Red Sea port of Jeddah, an escarpment suddenly rises sheer some 1,640 feet (500 m) out of the flat land, and from there the mountains, including the 10,827-foot (3,300-m) Jabal Sawda, stretch ruggedly all the way into Yemen in the south.

The central rocky plateau of the Najd with the capital Riyadh is traversed by a number of wadis, or dry river beds, and isolated by three great deserts from north, east, and south. In the north, the An Nafud covers about 21,236 square miles (55,000 sq. km) at an elevation of

Expansive red sands and spectacular sandstone rock formations in the Hisma desert, Tabuk region.

some 3,280 feet (1,000 m), mostly with longitudinal dunes scores of miles long, as much as 295 feet (90 m) high and separated by valleys as much as 10 miles (16 km) wide, given a reddish tinge at sundown by the iron ore in the sand. To the east runs the Ad Dahna, a narrow band of sand mountains also known as the River of Sand.

To the south of the Najd lies the mother of all deserts, the Rub al-Khali or Empty Quarter, which covers more than 212,356 square miles (550,000 sq. km) of wandering dunes at higher elevations and sandy flatlands and salt flats lower down. In its far southeast are the fabled quicksands said to have swallowed whole caravans. Most of it is totally without water and

Located in the Eastern Region, Al-Ahsa is the world's largest date oasis and a UNESCO World Heritage Site.

uninhabited—hence the name—except for a handful of wandering Bedouin and a minimal number of plant and animal species.

To the east of the Ad Dahna lies Al-Ahsa, the country's and indeed the world's largest date oasis, which in fact consists of two neighboring oases including the town of Al-Hofuf. It is on these fertile islands in the desert that the best of the Kingdom's dates are grown.

Saudi Arabia is bordered by Yemen and Oman in the south, the Red Sea in the west, Jordan and Iraq in the north, and Kuwait, the Persian Gulf, Qatar, and the United Arab Emirates (UAE) in the east. Across a causeway in the Gulf lies the island Kingdom of Bahrain, a popular weekend getaway destination for Saudis and expats alike.

CLIMATE

Most of the country has a desert climate, which means extreme dry heat during the day and abrupt temperature drops at night. In the Najd, temperatures rise commonly to 113°F (45°C) and can go as high as 129.2°F (54°C). This contrasts with the coastal areas of the Red Sea and the Persian Gulf, where the temperature only rises above 100.4°F (38°C) in the summer but humidity is usually more than 85 percent and often 100 percent. The winter is brief, and usually sees a few rain showers along the coast and even some rare and short-lived snowfall in northern and southern regions. Occasional snowfall can also be witnessed near Riyadh. Asir in the deep south experiences Indian Ocean monsoons, usually between October and March.

Overall, rainfall is low and erratic: it may consist of one or two torrential downpours for the entire year that flood the wadis and then rapidly disappear into the sand. Throughout most of the country the average rainfall is less than 6 inches (150 mm) per year, except for the southwestern region, where annual rainfall is between 15.7–23.6 inches (400–600 mm) per year. Entire regions may not see any rain at all for several years.

The Mega Aquifer System (MAS) is an ancient groundwater system and one of the world's largest aquifers, that runs under the driest deserts of Saudi Arabia and other countries of the Arabian Peninsula. However, it's always in danger of drying up due to the lack of rain replenishment. For much of the country today, water supply for human consumption and industrial use comes from huge desalination plants on the coast.

POPULATION

According to 2024 figures, there were some 36.4 million people living in the Kingdom, of whom about 13.4 million—nearly 40 percent—are foreigners. The highest numbers of expats are from India, Pakistan, Egypt,

A Saudi man wears a gold-trimmed *bisht* over his white *thobe*, signifying an important occasion.

Women in Riyadh wearing black *abayas* with *niqab* face coverings. Other head coverings include the *hijab* (pinned in place but face is fully visible) and *shayla* (a loose scarf that covers the hair).

Bangladesh, Yemen, the Philippines, Sudan, Nepal, and Syria. There are also increasing numbers of people from Europe, North and South America, the UK, Australia, and New Zealand.

Though it may come as a surprise, Saudis themselves are a diverse people and hail from a variety of ethnic backgrounds; a kaleidoscope of physical features can be seen when you spend time in the country. You'll meet many Saudis whose roots partially originate in other parts of the world, including Africa, the Indian subcontinent, and East Asia, as well as other parts of the Middle East.

When it comes to dress, Saudis at one time may have seemed a uniform people, with all men wearing the white *thobe*, a full-length robe, and women wearing a black *abaya*, a long gown. Modern-day Saudis, however, are comfortable in *thobes* of gray and dark blue, while *abayas* of all colors can be seen. Even more notable is the fact that women are no longer required to cover themselves from head to toe; as a result, a variety of dress styles is seen today that is often a combination of traditional and modern. The norms and expectations regarding dress are unpacked in greater detail in subsequent chapters.

Saudi Arabia consists of four distinct regions and populations. Each region has some nomadic and seminomadic elements: as recently as 1950, at least half the population were nomads. Tribal identities were at one time hugely important, but are becoming less central as Saudi society becomes more modern and urbanized. With 85 percent of the population living in urban areas and having adopted a metropolitan lifestyle, tribal lines have begun to blur and their significance has waned.

The Eastern Province, where the oil wealth is concentrated, has a substantial Shia population with cultural links to Iran, Bahrain, and other places in the Gulf region, as well as a component of Indian, Yemeni, and black African origins.

Asir in the south is in fact more closely linked to Yemen than to Saudi Arabia, both by population and its mountainous geography. This region is also home to the Flower Men (the Qahtani tribe), a small population who live in the mountains and who adorn their headbands with sprigs of wild flowers and cultivate perfume.

The Najd in the center is divided into three regions, with town centers that were quasi-independent city-states until the early twentieth century, some bitterly opposed to the ruling clan. Until development began in the 1960s, the Najd was relatively isolated, but its towns had populations linked to the Gulf, the Hijaz, and Africa.

The Hijaz on the west coast, home to the holy sites of Islam, was historically tied into the Ottoman bureaucratic system. The populations of Mecca, Medina, and Jeddah have for centuries been infused by descendants of foreign Muslims who came for the pilgrimage and stayed.

Mecca has substantial communities of Indian and Indonesian origin, and Jeddah has descendants of Persians and Hadramis (from Hadramaut or Aden in Yemen), as well as Africans and people from other parts of the Arabic-speaking world. Jeddah was the Kingdom's unrivaled commercial center until the 1960s, and in all the Hijaz towns, merchant families still form a powerful, liberal elite.

With diverse geographical backgrounds and multiple long-held, if now less prominent, tribal identities, what exactly unites modern-day Saudis? Well, three things principally: Islam, family values, and the Vision 2030.

Since long before national independence, the population of Saudi Arabia has been united under a set of deeply-rooted religious values that continues to permeate daily life and dictate almost every aspect of their culture and etiquette. We shall unpack the history and impact of Islam in Saudi Arabia, its birth place, and examine how it continues to play a dominant role in society today. Looking to the future, meanwhile, it is the monarchy and government's Vision 2030 that unites all Saudis toward a set of national goals that the country and all those who live in it are working toward, in one way or another. Whomever you talk to about the topic on the ground, whether young or old, the enthusiasm is clearly perceptible and, more often than not, they will take great pride in describing the national vision to you and the changes taking place in their society as a result. We look at the plan in greater detail later in this chapter.

A BRIEF HISTORY

Pre-Islamic Period

Arabs of the distant past were primarily herders, traders, and raiders, until a civilization developed in southern Arabia at around 1000 BCE. Small kingdoms or city-states—the best known is probably Saba, or Sheba in the Old Testament—were scattered across the land. The Romans called Yemen "Arabia Felix" (happy Arabia) because of its prosperity. Outside the coastal areas and a few centers in the Hijaz associated with the caravan trade, the harsh climate and desert limited agriculture and made the land difficult to access. The population in the hinterland probably subsisted on a combination of oasis gardening and herding, and most people were nomadic or seminomadic.

Cities that could service the camel caravans moving across the desert flourished. The most prosperous of these—Petra in Jordan and Palmyra in Syria—were close to the Mediterranean region, but small caravan cities developed on the Arabian peninsula as well. The most important was Mecca.

Some Arabs, particularly in the Hijaz, held religious beliefs that recognized multiple gods and rituals for worshiping them. They chiefly involved the sense that certain places and times of year were sacred. At those times, the near-permanent warfare between squabbling tribes, in particular, was forbidden, and various rituals were required. Foremost of these was the pilgrimage, and Mecca was the best-known pilgrimage site.

The Persians and the Romans were the great powers in the centuries before Islam, and the Arab tribes that lived near their territories were drawn into their political affairs. After 400 CE, both empires paid Arab tribes not only to protect their southern borders but also to harass the borders of their enemies. The time before Islam is generally referred to as *jahiliyya*, "the time of ignorance."

Early Islamic Period

Islam got off to a rocky start. When the Prophet Mohammed first began to preach this profoundly political religion, it angered his tribe, the Quraish, who controlled the pilgrimage traffic in Mecca and were custodians of the Kaaba, which was already the sacred shrine of a polytheistic religion and a pilgrimage destination. For Mohammed not only criticized such things as lax marriage arrangements, the treatment of women as chattels, and the killing of unwanted offspring, he also insisted there was only one God, thus potentially endangering the lucrative pilgrim traffic to the shrine.

In 615 Mohammed sent some of his followers to safety in Christian Ethiopia while he himself remained under siege in Mecca, but in 622 he fled to the town of Yatrib, some 200 miles (320 km) north of Mecca—his emigration marks the beginning of the Islamic calendar. He renamed the city Al-Madinah al-Munawarrah, the City of Light, now mostly known as Medina for short.

By 628, Mohammed had sufficient support to establish a truce with Mecca, finally conquering the city in 630 and smashing the three hundred and sixty idols in the Kaaba. He declared the territory surrounding the shrine *haram* (forbidden) to all non-Muslims, which it remains to this day. By his death in 632, Mohammed enjoyed the loyalty of almost all the tribes of Arabia.

Mohammed's successor, Abu Bakr, the first of the "rightly guided" caliphs, asked Mohammed's former secretary Zaid ibn Thabit to write down all the Prophet's revelations still in people's memories, producing a proto-Qur'an. The scriptures were passed to his successor, Umar, and his daughter, and under Umar's successor, Uthman, the same ibn Thabit produced a standardized, "authorized" version.

In the two years until his death, Abu Bakr maintained the loyalty of the Arab tribes by force, and in the battles that followed the Prophet's death—known as the apostasy wars—he enforced Islam across the peninsula. For the next thirty years, caliphs managed the growing Islamic empire from Medina.

With the end of the apostasy wars, the Arab tribes united behind Islam and turned their attention to the Roman and Persian empires. Arab-led armies pushed rapidly through both empires and in record time established Arab control from what is now Spain to Pakistan.

However, the empire soon ceased to be controlled from Arabia, whose importance declined. After the third caliph, Uthman, was assassinated in 656, the Muslim world was split into Sunni and Shia. The first regarded themselves as "people of the Sunnah," followers of the way in which the Prophet and his followers lived. The second believed that spiritual authority was conferred through the descendants of the fourth caliph, Ali, who spent much of his time in Iraq before he was murdered in 661 in Kufa.

After Ali, the Umayyads established a hereditary line of caliphs in Damascus until they were in turn overthrown in 750 by the Abbasids, who ruled from Baghdad. By the latter part of the eighth century, a mere two centuries after the birth of the Prophet, the political importance of Arabia in the Islamic world had declined.

THE PROPHET MOHAMMED

Mohammed was one of the most extraordinary men who ever lived. Born in 570 into the Quraish, the leading tribe in Mecca, he grew up illiterate and at twenty-five married Khadija, a wealthy widow fifteen years his senior who may have been his employer. Drawn to the monotheism of Jews and Christians, he withdrew to a cave to find the truth. In 610 he began to experience visitations of the angel Gabriel dictating to him the word of God; the resulting passages of masterful poetry, which he continued to produce throughout his life, were later collected from memory in the Qur'an—literally "recitations."

At first, Mohammed told only Khadija about his experiences, but in 613 he began to recite them publicly. Not surprisingly, his message of unity under one God was violently resisted by the pagan Meccans. Upon moving to Medina, Mohammed proved to be an astute leader. He contracted many alliances, often, after the death of his first wife, through marriage. The most famous was with Aisha, who was seven at the time but was to become his favorite and most influential wife. Aisha is the source of many *hadiths*, the traditions of the Prophet's sayings, that form part of the wider Islamic canon.

Mohammed expected but rarely forced pagans to submit to Islam, and allowed Christians and Jews—the "People of the Book"—to keep their faith provided they paid a special tax.

The Middle Ages

While Arabia became marginalized, Mecca remained the spiritual focus of Islam because it was the destination for the pilgrimage, while political importance lay in Medina. After the Prophet's death, Medina continued to be an administrative center and developed into an intellectual and literary one as well. In the seventh and eighth centuries, for instance, Medina became an important center for the legal discussions that would lead to the codification of Islamic law.

What is now Saudi Arabia became divided into two distinct regions. The Hijaz was variously controlled by whoever was powerful in the empire. In 1000, this was the Ismaili Fatimid dynasty, who ruled from their new capital, Cairo. In the thirteenth century, the Mamluk sultans of Egypt became the feudal overlords of the Hijaz, and in 1517 it passed to the Ottoman Empire after the Turks conquered Egypt. It also developed its cosmopolitan atmosphere due to the constant pilgrimage traffic.

The Najd, on the other hand, was more isolated and of no great importance to the imperial masters. This was chiefly due to its geographic location; once the Muslim empire spread, pilgrims from the west soon found more convenient routes that avoided the deserts.

KEY DATES

1744 Emir Mohammed ibn Saud and purist Islamic reformer Mohammed ibn Abdul Wahhab Al-Tamimi swear a holy oath to work together to establish a state run according to Islamic principles, with Abdul Wahhab in charge of religious matters and Mohammed ibn Saud in charge of politics. This marked the beginning of the first Saudi State in modern history.

1818 Ottoman forces, disturbed by the suppression of religious practices deemed heretical by Wahhabi authorities from the Hijaz to Iraq, invade Saudi territory across the Najd, capturing the Saudi stronghold at Diriya and executing leader Abdullah bin Saud.

1824 A second Saudi state was established in the Najd heartlands, with Riyadh established as the Wahhabi capital in 1830. This lasted until 1891, when the House of Saud was driven from the Najd by the rival Wahhabi Al-Rashid dynasty of Hail.

1912 Grandson of Abdullah bin Saud, Abdul Aziz (known popularly as Ibn Saud), who had fled with his family to Kuwait, returns with an army and conquers the Rashidi strongholds in the Najd. This marked the start of the third Saudi state.

1926 With British financial backing, Ibn Saud continues to wage war against the Ottoman-aligned Al Rashid in Najd as well as the Hashemite dynasty who had taken control of Mecca and the Hijaz. Upon defeating the Hashemites, Ibn Saud was declared King of the Hijaz.

1932 Ibn Saud unites his territories in the Najd and the Hijaz and proclaims the birth of the Kingdom of Saudi Arabia.

1938 Saudi Arabia discovers oil for the first time, a discovery that would forever change the economy and politics of the Middle East, and indeed the world.

1945 A fateful meeting between Ibn Saud and US President Franklin D. Roosevelt aboard the USS Quincy in the Suez Canal cements the budding alliance between the two countries. The deal effectively handed defense and regime security over to the USA and guaranteed a steady supply of cheap oil in return.

1953 Ibn Saud passes away and his second son, Saud, ascends to the throne. (Saud's elder brother, Prince Turki, had passed away of illness in 1919.)

1964 Saud abdicates the throne as a result of a *fatwa* (religious edict) and his younger brother Faisal becomes Saudi Arabia's new ruler. Often considered the start of the Kingdom's "Golden Age," King Faisal's reign sees the introduction of far-reaching reforms to the country, ranging from economy, government, and judiciary, to education, infrastructure, military, and health. King Faisal's progressive reforms brought the country great success, but it also drew him the ire of certain sections. King Faisal was assassinated during a *majlis* (a sit-in where citizens can personally petition the king) in Riyadh in 1975. He was succeeded by his half-brother, Khaled, as per Faisal's wishes.

1975 The period of King Khaled's reign saw the Saudi state cement its control over society and exert itself as a diplomatic power abroad. Increased oil revenues saw the country's wealth grow considerably and consolidating control over Aramco, thus renamed Saudi Aramco—Saudi's main oil extractor—saw Saudi become one of the richest countries in the world. King Khaled passed away in 1982.

1982 Upon Khaled's death, the crown is passed to King Fahd, Khaled's half-brother. His reign of twenty-five years—the longest in Saudi history—faced challenges early on when oil revenues dropped by 20 percent as the result of a global oil surplus. Fahd responded by diversifying the Saudi economy, developing industrial projects, creating joint ventures, and facilitating the introduction of advanced technology from abroad. He also introduced the Kingdom's Basic Law, a charter similar to a constitution, which included the creation of an advisory Shura Council that discusses and provides recommendations on new proposed laws, international agreements, and other issues regarding the welfare of the Saudi people. Despite suffering a stroke in 1995 he continued to rule for another ten years.

2005 King Abdullah ascends the throne and embarks on far-reaching reforms including on the standing of women in Saudi society. During his reign, a law was enacted that requires 20 percent of the Shura Council to be made up of women, he legalized the vote for women in municipal elections, and permitted female athletes to compete in the Olympics for the Saudi national team. He also introduced numerous initiatives in the field of education, including the introduction of the Custodian of the Two Holy Mosques Scholarship Program that sends thousands of young Saudi men and women to study abroad every year.

King Salman bin Abdulaziz Al Saud

King Salman is the current king of Saudi Arabia at the time of publication, who ascended to the throne in 2015 at age 79. He has played a key role in shaping the country's policies on economic diversification, social reforms, and regional diplomacy. The King, along with his son, Crown Prince Mohammed Bin Salman, work in partnership on many projects, including the grand Vision 2030 (see page 35).

King Salman served as the Governor of Riyadh from 1963 to 2011 and played a key role in developing the city from a medium-sized town into the metropolis that it is today. To this end, he fostered and developed

King Salman bin Abdulaziz Al Saud.

economic and political relationships with Western leaders and oversaw the construction of new universities, schools, and sports stadiums.

As king, he is credited with streamlining bureaucracy and reducing the government secretariats from eleven to two: the Council of Political and Security Affairs and the Council for Economic and Development Affairs. An active philanthropist, he made large-scale donations to Syrian and Rohingya refugees and many other relief projects through the King Salman Center for Relief and Humanitarian Aid (KSRelief). During his reign, the execution of convicted minors was abolished.

Mohammed bin Salman Al Saud (MBS)

Popularly known as MBS, Mohammed bin Salman Al Saud is the Crown Prince and Prime Minister. Born in 1985, he is King Salman's seventh son and was the firstborn of the king's third wife, Fahda bint Falah Al Hithlain.

Mohammed studied law at King Saud University and began his career in politics in 2007, when he was appointed as an advisor to the Council of Ministers. In 2009 he was appointed as an advisor to his father, then the governor of Riyadh. He quickly moved up the ranks and was subsequently appointed to a number of ministerial positions, including the minister of defense and the position of deputy crown prince in 2015.

Crown Prince Mohammed bin Salman Al Saud, otherwise known as MBS.

MBS enjoys widespread popularity, although a small minority has reservations about his many reforms. Some do not like that he has taken steps to limit the power of the clergy, nor that he has opened Saudi Arabia up to mass tourism and invited major Western music and sports stars to the Kingdom. Many more support the stance he has taken against corruption and the furthering of women's rights, such as by abolishing their driving ban in 2018, limiting the role of the *mutawwa* religious police, and ending gender segregation in public spaces. MBS and his father, King Salman, together are the masterminds behind the country's revolutionary development plan, Vision 2030.

THE POLITICAL SYSTEM

Saudi Arabia is an absolute monarchy. The king, from the House of Saud, holds executive powers overseeing the Council of Ministers and the authority to make final decisions on all matters of governance, law, and foreign policy. The Shura Council acts as an advisory body to the king, while the *ulema* constitutes the Kingdom's religious authority.

The *ulema,* honoring the original Saudi-Wahhabi pact, is led by the Grand Mufti who is a direct descendent of Mohammed ibn Abdul Wahhab. Though political parties are prohibited, there has been a shift in recent years toward increased public participation, such as through municipal elections.

The legal system is based on Shariah law, which in the Kingdom relies on the Hanbali *fiqh*, one of the four legal schools in Islam. There are several hundred Shariah courts around the country as well as some special tribunals established by decree, such as the Labor Court, and two appeals courts in Riyadh and Mecca. The minister of justice, appointed by the king from among the most senior *ulema*, is the de facto chief justice.

The Council of Ministers, the government's cabinet, is made up of twenty-three ministers with portfolios and seven ministers of state. All members of the council are appointed by royal decree. The crown prince serves as both prime minister and chairman of the Council of Ministers under the leadership of the king.

THE ECONOMY

Saudi Arabia was a subsistence economy until the 1930s when, in conjunction with Standard Oil Company of California, enormous oil reserves were discovered. Today, Saudi Arabia is the world's largest oil exporter and holds the world's second-largest proven oil reserves, at 266.5 billion barrels. In 2023, production output was measured at 10.36 million barrels per day (bpd), down from a peak of 12.0 million bpd in April 2020. At current production levels, the Kingdom's oil reserve is forecast to last for approximately another sixty years.

The oil reserves are located mostly in the Eastern Province, home to the giant government-owned oil corporation Saudi Aramco that functions almost as a state within a state. The lifeblood of the country, oil

An offshore oil and gas rig near the coastal city of Dammam.

exports currently account for 46 percent of GDP, with China, Japan, South Korea, India, and the US being the five largest consumers of Saudi oil. Being the world's largest oil exporter ensures the Kingdom far-reaching political leverage in international affairs; an increase or decrease in production holds vital consequence for the global economy by way of increasing or reducing inflationary pressure on the economies of friends and foe alike.

The Kingdom also has vast reserves of natural gas, totaling around 298 trillion cubic feet, which is enough to last for over one hundred years at current consumption levels. In addition to oil and natural gas, Saudi Arabia also has significant reserves of other minerals including gold, silver, copper, and uranium.

Beyond the energy sector and associated industries, Saudi Arabia's service sector accounts for roughly 53 percent of GDP. Approximately 3 percent of GDP is constituted by the agricultural sector, the most important exports of which are dates, wheat, barley, sorghum, tomatoes, watermelons, eggplants, potatoes, cucumbers, and onions. The main markets for Saudi agricultural goods are the United Arab Emirates, Yemen, Pakistan, Sudan, and India.

In 2023, the labor force totaled approximately 16 million workers, approximately 6 million of whom were expat workers. The labor force participation rate of Saudis was at 52.5 percent, with 8 percent unemployment.

With the country's finances so heavily reliant on a single finite resource, the Kingdom is making great

effort to diversify its economy in the coming decades
and so as to secure its viability and continued success.
Enter Vision 2030 …

VISION 2030

The Saudi Vision 2030 is a grand scheme launched
by King Salman and Crown Prince Mohammed
bin Salman in 2016 that has three central goals: the
transformation of the Kingdom's economy from one that
is dependent on oil to one that is diversified, forward
looking, and that taps into the country's largest as yet

The Line: a linear smart city currently under construction in the northwestern Tabuk Region. As part
of the NEOM Giga Project, the city is designed to have no cars and no carbon emissions.

untapped resource: its people; the development of a vibrant, healthy, and fulfilling society that is founded on a modern and moderate Islamic identity; and improving all governmental and bureaucratic services by increasing transparency, efficiency, and accountability. These goals seek to fundamentally develop the way that Saudi society is set up and run. Its goals and strategies for achieving this are far-reaching and will affect all aspects of life in Saudi Arabia. Indeed, many already are.

Economic Diversification

Considering the imperative, the initiatives being implemented to wean the country's economy from its dependency on its finite oil reserves are remarkable both in scale and ingenuity. Without putting too fine a point on it, it's hard to think of another country on earth that is currently undergoing strategic structural change to put into practice so clear a vision of what its future will look like. At a time when many countries around the world struggle for strategic coherency from one government to the next, this is an example of forward planning par excellence. The stakes are high; the future of the Kingdom depends on the success of these projects, no less.

So what does the Saudi economy look like under the Vision 2030 plan? Well, the most tangible examples are to be found in the Giga Projects: a range of grand scale developments each designed to stimulate the economy in a variety of ways, from generating new employment opportunities, to developing both new and existing sectors such as tourism and sustainable energy, the development of infrastructure, eradicating corruption from its business and bureaucratic spheres, and the development of the country's scientific and cultural fields, all of which in turn will promote and foster new economic activity and foreign investment.

The flagship Giga Project is NEOM, a $500 billion mega-city that once completed will cover 10,200 square miles (26,500 square kilometers). To put things into perspective, that's roughly thirty-three times the size of New York City. This "Land of the Future" will run wholly on renewable energy and aims to become an international hub for a range of services and sectors. The architects of the project that is funded by PIF, the Saudi national fund,

Under construction: Qiddiya Entertainment City. A Giga Project creating the Kingdom's "capital of entertainment" some 45 minutes from Riyadh.

describe the development as "a vision of what a new future might look like." It is designed to become a sustainable ecosystem for living and working, and its success would constitute a global achievement. Other Giga Projects and subsidiary projects include the development of vast and unique tourism and entertainment sites such as the Red Sea Global and Qiddiya Entertainment City.

Regional Headquarters

Announced in February 2021, this initiative, also known as Program HQ, mandates that all companies wishing to do business with the government of Saudi Arabia must have relocated their regional headquarters to Riyadh by January 1, 2024.

The policy was designed to promote the country's economic growth and to transform Riyadh, currently a city of approximately eight million inhabitants, to a regional business hub. The policy includes many incentives for international companies that take part, including a fifty-year tax holiday, exemption from the "Saudization" policies for ten years (see below), and more.

Saudization

The Saudi Nationalization Scheme, or Saudization, is designed to reduce the country's reliance on foreign workers and increase the number of Saudi nationals active in the workforce. The measures adopted to achieve this include the introduction of quotas in both public and private sectors requiring a certain percentage of the workforce to be of Saudi origin. Companies are also required to provide training and development

The King Abdullah Financial District (KAFD) in Riyadh's Al-Aqeeq neighborhood.

opportunities to their Saudi employees and so take part in the national project of upskilling the local workforce. Job centers have been established across the country by the government to help locals find employment or enroll in training programs. Meanwhile, incentives have been introduced for multinational companies that employ Saudis, including subsidies and tax breaks, and advantages when bidding for government contracts. Finally, in some industries, such as retail and hospitality, the government has implemented a quota limit on the proportion of foreign workers permitted, in order to encourage the sourcing of local staff and personnel.

Developments in Saudi Society

In addition to economic development, Vision 2030 also includes initiatives that are aimed at improving the quality of life for Saudi citizens through large-scale investment in healthcare, education, infrastructure, housing, sports, and entertainment.

As part of these improvements, the Vision aims to improve the efficiency and effectiveness of the country's governmental and bureaucratic services. This includes reducing red tape, introducing new technologies to streamline operations, and increasing transparency. There has also been a major crackdown on corruption in recent years. To this end, the Saudi government established Nazaha, the Control and Anti-Corruption authority, which has a hotline and reporting system for corruption in government and private sectors.

By investing in infrastructure, upskilling its workforce, clamping down on corruption, and improving the quality of life of its residents and citizens, Saudi hopes to position itself as an attractive and competitive environment for foreign investment, a vital goal of its Vision.

The changes made in the last few years have been dramatic. Young Saudis are growing up in a society that is markedly different to the one in which their parents grew up. Ask foreign expatriates living and working in the Kingdom—or those who lived here in the past and later returned—what they make of the changes of recent years and you will, for the most part, hear variations of the same answer: "Everything has changed, and changed for the better."

Social Change

A country that used to be highly secretive and closed off to the rest of the outside world is becoming a very different place under the Vision 2030. We wouldn't have a complete understanding of the changes being made as part of the Vision without touching on some of the social changes that are underway as part of the plan.

One of the most significant changes, especially in the eyes of the international community, has been the changes to the lives of Saudi women. The lifting of the ban on women driving, increased access to education and employment opportunities, improved healthcare services, and expanded women's rights are the focal points of these changes.

Recognizing that there was a need for increased participation of women in the workforce, the government has introduced several policies and initiatives which include allowing women to drive, a law which came into place on June 24, 2018. The government has also introduced policies to increase job opportunities for women in both the public and private sectors, setting a target of increasing the percentage of women in the workforce from 22 percent to 30 percent by 2030.

To this end, numerous training and development programs have been introduced, while the private sector has been encouraged to implement flexible working hours to help women balance their home and work lives. For more on changes to the position of women in Saudi society, see page 59.

For the first time, Saudi is also seeing the establishment of theaters, cinemas, and music and arts festivals that have breathed new life into the country's cultural landscape. A vibrant cultural scene is emerging, one that fosters social cohesion in a way that wasn't tangible before (see Chapter 6).

Sports and recreational exercise are being developed as the Kingdom strives to enhance the physical well-being of its populace. This is no easy feat in a country where average temperatures regularly reach 100°F (40°C) and that has not traditionally engaged in regular physical activity as a pastime. To encourage people to take part in sporting activities, state-of-the-art facilities have been constructed both to provide venues of practice but also to host national and international tournaments. These initiatives are creating a sense of national pride, encouraging active lifestyles, and nurturing local sporting talent.

As part of the Vision 2030 initiative, the Kingdom has modernized its healthcare facilities, enhanced the quality of education, developed affordable housing, and implemented social support programs with a view to increase the standard of living and satisfaction of its citizens.

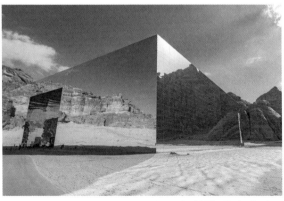

The mirrored Maraya Concert Hall in the ancient oasis of Al-Ula, Medina Province.

The Mutawa

In the past, Islamic traditions and Sharia Law were strictly enforced by the *mutawa*, or religious police. Before 2016, when for women covering one's head and hair in public was still compulsory, the *mutawa* would approach uncovered women in public and instruct them to cover their hair. In the past, all Saudi women were also required to have a male guardian (*wali*), usually either their father, husband, a brother, or close male relative, present at all times with them in public. This custom, common in Saudi Arabia for centuries, was practiced to ensure that the honor of the woman and family were not harmed as they would have been if a single woman was seen consorting with men of another family, regardless of the circumstances. In 2019, the guardianship law was partially amended and now only applies to women under the age of twenty-one. Before the amendment, the *mutawa* would commonly approach couples or mixed-gender groups to ask about their relationship and why they were together. It could be a disconcerting experience, as they would often ask to see documents proving you were either married or related to the people of the opposite gender in your company, and there would be consequences if you could not.

Nowadays the role of the *mutawa* has shifted from that of an enforcement body to that of an advisory and educational institution. They no longer have duties of public enforcement, but instead fulfill a role based on providing guidance, which aligns with the Vision's broader goal of creating a more inclusive and respectful society for all.

CHAPTER TWO

VALUES & ATTITUDES

ISLAM

It's impossible to imagine Saudi Arabia without Islam for it is both at the core of what is most important to people and provides the shape and substance of their daily lives. From public debate to art and architecture, almost everything in Saudi Arabia is predicated on, and circumscribed by, Islam.

The Kingdom's western Hijaz region is home to Mecca (the birthplace of the Prophet Mohammed) and its sister city, Medina, which form the destination for the great annual pilgrimage, or Hajj. Saudi Arabia's unique position as home to its two holiest cities makes it the cradle of Islam, and the proud custodian and servant of the holy sites.

The sometimes fearful preconceptions of Western visitors whose only interaction with the world's second largest religion is via news reports of attacks carried out by extremists is greatly unfortunate. On visiting

Saudi, your introduction to and interaction with the living tradition of Islam will hopefully allow you to know it more intimately. You will find that it is welcoming and hospitable, has much to say about life, and much to offer in the human conversation on values and our place in the universe.

It is worth noting too that extremist views are not supported by the vast majority of Muslims around the world. Indeed, it may come as a surprise that Islam, being the youngest sibling in the family of Abrahamic religions (the other two being Christianity and Judaism), shares many of the stories and venerated figures of its two older siblings. Both Christians and Jews, upon reading the Qur'an, find they know a surprising portion of the stories for this reason.

As when visiting any country, showing respect for the host culture gives birth to the space where real meeting and interaction can take place. Saudi Arabia is no different, and while Saudis will make great exceptions for foreigners who do not know their culture, due to the conservative nature of its society, brushing up on local norms is a good idea, particularly if you don't wish to cause inadvertent offence. Learning about these norms, why they exist, and how to partake of them will allow you to meet Saudis on their own terms.

The Five Pillars of Islam

The Five Pillars of Islam have a rich historical and cultural background that dates back to the time of the Prophet Mohammed. They are considered the essential elements of the Muslim faith, and are a testament to the devotion and commitment of Muslims to their religion. The pillars

Worshipers gather for prayer at Al-Masjid an Nabawi in Medina, Islam's second holiest mosque.

provide a framework for Muslims to practice their faith, and they are a source of inspiration and guidance for millions of people around the world.

The first pillar of Islam, the Shahada, is the declaration that a Muslim must make in order to become a member of the faith. It is a simple statement that there is no God but Allah and that Mohammed is his prophet. This declaration is considered to be the foundation of the Muslim faith and is recited by Muslims throughout the day.

The second pillar of Islam is Salah, or prayer. Muslims are required to pray five times a day, facing toward Mecca. The prayer is performed at specific times throughout the day and is intended to show submission to Allah and to remind Muslims of their faith.

When in Saudi Arabia, it's a good idea to get used to the call to prayer which rings out from mosques five times a day. At prayer time, it's common to see people stop their car at the nearest mosque or rushing there on foot. They may even pray on the street outside or, if driving, may stop on the side of the road and lay out their prayer mat in the sand, facing Mecca. If you are working in Saudi Arabia, it's advisable to become familiar with the prayer times and so try not to schedule meetings or other engagements during those times. If an event does overlap prayer time, try to plan a break into the schedule to allow time for prayer. For practical help on prayer times, which change slightly every day, you can download a prayer time app of which there are numerous to choose from.

Most shops and government offices close during prayer times, and people will stop whatever they are doing in order to pray. However, there is also flexibility in prayer and some people will pray slightly before or after the prescribed time, depending on their work-related demands.

The third pillar of Islam is Zakat, or giving to charity. Muslims are required to give a portion of their wealth to the less fortunate, as a way of showing compassion and generosity toward others. This act of giving is considered to be an important part of the Muslim faith and is seen as a way of purifying one's wealth and earning blessings from Allah.

The fourth pillar of Islam is Sawm, or fasting during the holy month of Ramadan. During this time, Muslims refrain from eating and drinking from *fajr* prayer before dawn until dusk, as a way of showing devotion to Allah and reminding themselves of the suffering of the less fortunate. The fast is broken each day with a meal called *iftar*, which is often shared with friends and family.

The fifth and final pillar of Islam is Hajj, or pilgrimage to Mecca. Muslims who are physically and financially able are required to make the pilgrimage to Mecca at least once in their lifetime. The Hajj is a symbolic journey that is meant to connect Muslims with their faith and with the history of their religion.

Zamzam water

Zamzam water is a sacred water source in Islam, located in Mecca. It is believed to have originated thousands of years ago when Hagar, the wife of Ibrahim, and their son Ismail were in the desert and in search of water. Hagar walked seven times between the hills of Safa and Marwah looking for water. In one version of the narrative, the angel Gabriel (Jibra'il) then came and revealed the source of water; in another version young Ismail struck the ground with his foot, and the water from Zamzam sprang forth.

Zamzam water holds special significance for Muslims and is considered to be a blessing from Allah. It's believed to have healing properties and is often used for drinking, cooking, and washing. Many believe that drinking Zamzam water can bring about spiritual and physical benefits and it is often sought after by pilgrims during the Hajj and Umrah pilgrimages to Mecca.

Zamzam water is also the subject of many stories and legends in Islamic tradition, with some believers

Zamzam water being poured from a copper jug.

recounting miraculous experiences they have had after drinking it. Its properties cannot be understood even through the lens of modern science.

RELIGION AND STATE

While Islam is the state religion, the practice of Islam varies greatly according to the interpretation and tradition of its followers. In Saudi Arabia, the dominant form of Islam belongs to the Sunni tradition known as Wahhabism, which forms the basis for the state's ideology. It is named after Mohammed ibn Abdul Wahhab (1703–92 CE), the religious reformer born in the Najd region of Saudi, who formed the power-sharing alliance with the House of Saud that lasts to this day.

Simplicity plays a crucial role in Wahhabism and serves to uphold the fundamental tenets of the faith and maintain a pure connection with Allah. The belief system, worship practices, and lifestyle choices of Wahhabi adherents reflect the emphasis on simplicity.

One of its key features was the segregation of men and women enforced across the Kingdom, especially in the Najd and its capital Riyadh. This has been somewhat relaxed in recent years, but gender-separated lines are still found at the airport and public offices, as well as seating sections of restaurants and cafés.

More broadly, Wahhabism stresses the "oneness" of God, or *tawhid,* and emphasizes the Prophet Mohammed as the last prophet of God.

Meanwhile, Saudi Arabia's Shia population constitutes about 10 to 15 percent of the total population. Determining the exact figure is complicated by the sensitivity of sectarian demographics in the country and the limited availability of official data.

The regional geopolitical landscape is greatly influenced by the Sunni-Shia divide and tensions between Saudi Arabia and Iran, the two main flag-bearers of each tradition, has affected the treatment of the local Shia population. Saudi Arabia views Iran not simply as a regional rival but as a threat to the Kingdom's existence, owing to the radical ideology of its post-revolution Ayatollahs. In recent years, however, the Saudi government has taken concrete steps to address the concerns of its Shia minority and improve their treatment. For example, efforts have been made to provide greater political representation, improve access to education and employment, and curb discrimination based on religious affiliation.

The Kingdom is governed by Shariah, or Islamic law, which serves as the foundation for legislation and governance in the country. That said, the Kingdom has undertaken several reforms aimed at modernizing its legal system and promoting social progress. Life in the Kingdom has always been influenced by the delicate balance between the country's two main power centers: the ruling monarchy, who must balance the country's political and economic needs, and which includes a liberal and highly educated elite among branches of its broad royal family, and the strict ideology of the Wahhabi *ulema* (religious council). The power balance between these poles has fluctuated over the years and has shifted further from the *ulema* under MBS.

Among the most notable changes that have been implemented are those regarding women's rights, particularly the reforms concerning male guardianship. For example, women now have the autonomy to travel, obtain passports, and access government services without the permission of a male guardian. They can also now move around in public freely without a male guardian, including driving their own car. While many in the West and elsewhere may take these rights for granted, observers should note that these changes have taken place over a very short space of time relative to how things have been here both before the country's independence and after. More on changes to the position of women can be found on page 59.

In terms of criminal law, in 2020 the Saudi Arabian Supreme Court announced the abolition of flogging, or lashing, as a form of punishment. It has been replaced with alternative penalties such as imprisonment, fines, or community service. Saudi has also introduced laws in 2018 that criminalized sexual harassment, providing legal protection, and remedies for victims.

Several reforms have also been made to the law surrounding marriage. For example, now there are processes put into place to regulate the process of marriage by introducing standardized marriage contracts. The goal is to ensure transparency, protect women's rights, and reduce instances of forced or exploitative marriages. The legal age for marriage has also been raised to eighteen years for both males and females (exceptions may be granted by a judge in certain circumstances). Specialized family courts have been set up to handle family-related disputes, such as divorce, custody, and inheritance matters.

The consumption of alcohol is prohibited, and men can have up to four wives, as long as he has the means to support all of them financially. In reality, having multiple wives is pretty rare and most men choose monogamy.

The sentence for a number of crimes including murder, sodomy, and witchcraft is death by public beheading, though a murder can be redeemed by the payment of "blood money" (*diyah*) to the victim's family. Public executions have reduced dramatically in recent years, from 154 in 2016 to 27 in 2021. (By way of comparison, 17 people were executed in the US in 2021.)

In Saudi Arabia, the practice of religions other than Islam is not allowed. Nonetheless, it's important to note that in recent years, there have been some steps toward religious tolerance and interfaith dialogue. There have even been several international conferences aimed at fostering understanding and promoting peaceful coexistence among different religious communities. One such event was the World Conference on Dialogue in 2008, organized in Madrid by the Muslim World League from Mecca, in which it hosted 200 participants from all over the world representing Islam, Christianity, Judaism, Buddhism, and other religions. Then in 2012, Saudi Arabia along with Austria, Spain, and the Vatican formed the King Abdullah bin Abdulaziz International Center for Interreligious and Interfaith Dialogue (KAICIID) in Vienna, Austria to increase the opportunities for peaceful dialogue amongst different faiths.

These efforts reflect a desire to engage with the international community on open dialogue about religions, focusing not on what's different but what is shared amongst the religions. Most importantly, the efforts address how people of different faiths can respect each other and live in harmony together. All of these initiatives reveal a Saudi Arabia which is becoming more moderate and exclusive. On its own soil (sand), Saudi Arabia has made efforts in combating extremism and has taken measures to protect the rights of non-Muslims living in Saudi Arabia, especially in designated private compounds and diplomatic areas, where non-Muslims are allowed to practice their faith in private.

However, it's crucial to remember that the *public* practice of religions other than Islam, including the construction of non-Muslim places of worship, officially remains prohibited in Saudi Arabia. Non-Muslim religious materials, such as Bibles or religious symbols, must not be displayed *in public*.

The point to remember if you are visiting or living in Saudi Arabia is that whatever beliefs, practices, or traditions you have, or religion or school of thought you belong to, it should be kept private. As long as you don't publicize what you are doing or try to convert others, you are in line with the law. What you do inside your home is your private, personal business and as long as it is not in the public eye, you are safe in continuing your practices.

In any case, since the situation is always evolving, it's important to consult official sources or reputable news outlets for the most accurate and up-to-date information on religious practices and regulations in Saudi Arabia.

TRIBAL LOYALTIES

Saudi Arabia was historically a tribal society characterized by deep-rooted structures of loyalty, affiliation, and protection. While tribal identities are becoming less prominent today as Saudi transforms into a modern, cosmopolitan society, it is still important to understand what they mean and how they operate. Traditionally, loyalties in Saudi society operated in concentric circles, starting with the family, followed by the tribe, friends, the nation, the Muslim ummah (community), and then the rest. These loyalties would often take precedence over contractual obligations or political affiliations, and to some extent this is still the case. Urban Saudis in the country's rapidly growing cities, however, are gradually shifting away from strict tribal affiliations, and local or class associations are beginning to replace age-old familial loyalties as societal structures evolve. For them, tribal heritage is a source of pride and can still bring benefits in certain situations.

Saudi tribes trace their origins to various Arabian Peninsula regions and historical migrations. The heartland of Saudi Arabia, Najd, is home to many prominent tribes, including the Al-Saud clan, the ruling family of Saudi Arabia, and Al-Rashid, Al-Utaybah, and Al-Murrah. The Hijaz region on the west coast of the country, which includes the cities of Mecca and Medina, is associated with tribes such as the Hashemites, the ruling family of Jordan, and the Al-Sharif family. The Asir region in the southern part of Saudi Arabia is home to tribes such as the Al-Ghamdi, Al-Muharib, and Al-Harith. The Eastern Province, known for its oil reserves, is inhabited by tribes such as the Al-Dosari, Al-Otaibi, and Al-Jarrah.

Throughout history, tribes in the Arabian Peninsula have migrated and mixed with each other, making it challenging to pinpoint exact origins. Some tribes have Bedouin roots, associated with nomadic lifestyles and desert regions, while others have settled in specific areas for generations. The tribal landscape of Saudi Arabia is indeed complex, with numerous tribes spread across the country. Each tribe often has its own unique history, traditions, and genealogy. There are also many Saudis whose families settled there from other parts of the Muslim world and were given citizenship in the early days of the Kingdom. With surnames like Al-Hindi (meaning from India) or Al-Maghribi (from the Maghrib, or North Africa).

The influence of tribes remains significant in social life, with members maintaining strong connections even when living abroad. Expatriate Saudis remain closely connected to their homeland and will keep track of events and gatherings within their tribe.

Saudi television frequently broadcasts live meetings between the king and tribal leaders, highlighting the importance of demonstrating loyalty to the ruling family. The televised meetings also show that tribal leaders have the king's ear should there arise a need for mediation. Tribal sheikhs will often publicly express their commitment to the king and country, particularly after events that may be seen as divisive.

HONOR

Honor holds significant importance in Saudi Arabia, where it is crucial for men and women to uphold honorable behavior in their daily lives. The concept of honor permeates Saudi society, influencing interpersonal dynamics, social interactions, and the perception of one's identity. This includes refraining from theft, being a generous host, practicing one's faith, and fulfilling one's roles as a provider or supporter. One notable aspect of Saudi society is the relatively low crime rate, where forgotten items are often found untouched even days later.

Any perceived damage to a person or family's honor is taken very seriously. Insulting a man's parentage or the conduct of his mother is particularly hurtful and can provoke strong reactions. Respect and its outward expression play a crucial role in Saudi society across various relationships, from young to old, guest to host, and business partner to business partner. In conflicts or disagreements, shouting and references to wounded honor are common tactics, often employed to gain leverage in a heated argument, and saving face becomes paramount.

FAMILY AND PRIVACY

Aside from Islam, family is the central focus of most people's lives in Saudi. It's common for several generations to live under one roof, though younger Saudis today increasingly like to branch out on their own. Much of Saudi social interaction takes place within the family and privacy is valued, as evidenced by the high walls that often surround houses, or the shaded windows of city-center apartments. Overall, Saudis are intensely private people and the family home is sacrosanct—people do not turn up uninvited. In addition, people will not intrude on the private space of a visitor, either.

With family playing such a central role in people's private and social lives, it makes sense that many public entertainment options are geared toward families, too. Restaurants, for example, usually have a "family only" section where they can eat together hidden from the intrusive glances of outsiders.

WOMEN IN SOCIETY

A lot has changed for women in Saudi Arabia in recent years, particularly since the launch of Vision 2030, which saw numerous legal provisions introduced toward increasing the personal autonomy of women and raising their position in society.

At the outset, in order to understand the Saudi perspective, it's important to understand that what is widely thought of by the Western world as the oppression of women, in Saudi Arabia is considered as a system of protection based on Sharia law.

As time has changed, and the pragmatism of the leadership has allowed it to acknowledge the untapped potential of nearly half of its population, a relaxation of the application of Sharia principles has meant marked change in numerous areas, toward the goal of national development that is so vital to the Kingdom's Vision 2030.

Guardianship

One key area of change has been in the area of male guardianship. The implications of guardianship in Saudi were far-reaching; essentially, all decision-making powers regarding a woman's life, from education and marriage, to travel and socializing, were legally assigned to a male guardian, usually a close male family member or spouse.

In 2001, the law changed to grant women the right to their own identification documents; before that, they were listed on the papers of their father or husband. In 2015, women were granted the right to vote and run in municipal elections. It was 2018 when a ban on driving was lifted, and in 2019 the leadership introduced a raft of changes to the country's guardianship laws. Women twenty-one years of age and above were now allowed to obtain passports for themselves and their children, and were permitted to travel abroad without prior approval or a male guardian present. Women may now also register any official changes in status like marriage, divorce, births, and deaths without the approval of a male guardian.

It's helpful to understand the seismic shift these changes represent. In traditional Saudi society, it was considered to bring shame on a man if his wife or sister's name was uttered in public. To alert girls when school is out that the guardian who has come to pick them up has arrived at the gates, for example, he would call out his own name over the public-address system. Women who have given birth are commonly referred to as Umm (mother of), followed by the name of their firstborn, say Umm Mohammed, rather than their given name.

Men were also not allowed to know the names of females connected to his family by marriage, such as in-laws or his friends' wives. In a family WhatsApp group, for example, the wives of brothers in the same family would not be included, since that would render their names and numbers visible to other male members of the family. Still today, it is common for women to not talk to or show their faces to their husband's friends or her brothers-in-law. This is less strictly adhered to in urban areas, but there are still many traditional people who do follow this custom.

Even now, Saudi men will rarely discuss their wives when conversing about family. They will talk about their kids, parents, brothers, and sisters, or their family in a general sense, but wives are still considered a private topic. As such, visitors and expats should take care not to ask about a man's wife specifically. If an expat develops a close relationship with Saudi friends or colleagues, and Saudis mention their wives, it's okay to engage in conversation about them. When having dinner with a Saudi couple, men should take care not to talk in unequal proportions with the man's wife.

Women's Dress
Laws requiring women to cover themselves have long garnered criticism from the outside world, with much

of the international community seeing it as a form of oppression. Within Saudi Arabia, however, and much of the Muslim world, it is seen as a means for a woman to protect her honor. The legal changes introduced in recent years have affected this issue, too. As of 2018, women are no longer legally required to wear an *abaya*—the traditional long gown which can be any color, but usually black—or the *hijab*, which is wrapped around the head and neck.

In addition to the *abaya* and *hijab*, there is also the *niqab*, a black cloth that covers the face except for the eyes, and the *gata*, a veil that covers the whole face. In strict observance of Sharia law, some women will also wear black gloves to cover their hands.

Interestingly, despite the changes in law, most women in Saudi still opt to wear at least part—or all—of the traditional dress and it speaks to the competing social forces that are at play in modern Saudi. It is estimated that as many as 80 percent of women prefer to wear some combination of the *abaya* and *hijab*. If you ask most Saudi women why they choose to do so, you will hear a number of reasons: many will say that it is down to personal preference, though how much that is influenced by long-standing social norms is hard to say. Others wear it out of a conscious intention to continue the tradition: their mothers and grandmothers wore it and for that reason they want to continue to wear it, too. Still others will cite their desire to keep themselves covered until marriage, and therefore unseen by any man before their husband.

Generally speaking, the majority of expat women working in Saudi also continue to wear an *abaya* when out in public, though not a *hijab*. In most office environments it's not necessary to wear an *abaya*. In fact, many who do wear it while traveling to and from work will hang the garment up once inside their office, much like a jacket. More on work dress codes can be found in Chapter 8.

Education

Public education for girls, on a voluntary basis, was introduced in 1960, by King Faisal and his wife Queen Effat—an elite private girls' institute in Jeddah that is probably the closest the Kingdom has to a Western-style liberal arts college is named after her. Today, school is compulsory for both girls and boys at primary level for six years.

In 2023, women made up 52 percent of students enrolled at public universities, and the government has launched initiatives to both improve the quality of education and increase enrollment of women into higher education.

Women in Work

In the not-so-distant past, work and business in the Kingdom was a man's world. Many recent initiatives, including the National Transformation Program, aim to provide women with more job opportunities, improve workplace conditions, and promote entrepreneurship, in order to increase the women's labor force participation rate to 30% by 2030. Women are now able to work in a wide range of industries and professions, including traditionally male-dominated sectors like engineering and finance. The government has also introduced legal reforms aimed at increasing women's rights in the workplace, and mandating equal pay for equal work, as well as laws prohibiting gender discrimination or the dismissal of women while on maternity leave.

As a result, women are increasingly taking on leadership positions in private and public sector jobs, particularly in finance, healthcare, and education. National and international news outlets have taken notice of the vast uptake of women in the professional world of Saudi Arabia. One such example from a BBC news headline in February 2022 read: "28,000 women apply for 30 train operator jobs in Saudi Arabia."

Women also now have government support and new regulations in place allowing them to open new businesses and manage them personally without the need for prior approval from a male guardian to do so. Under the National Entrepreneurship Initiative and the establishment of the Small and Medium Enterprises Authority, women are encouraged to start their own businesses, and there are now several support programs available specifically for female entrepreneurs. Through the encouragement of female entrepreneurship, the world of business in Saudi Arabia is witnessing a surge in growth. In 2022, the General Authority for Small and Medium enterprises (Monsha'at) released a report that revealed that women-owned business accounted for 45 percent of all start-ups in Saudi Arabia that year. This statistic goes a long way to illustrate the industrious and entrepreneurial spirit of Saudi women today, who, having now been given the chance, are working hard to make their mark and contribute to the betterment of their society and the wider world.

Sports

As part of the social reforms established to promote gender equality came the lifting of the ban on women attending sports events. In addition, women are now able to participate in numerous national sports events, including the 2018 World Squash Championships and the 2019 Dakar Rally, which for the first time included a category for female drivers.

In 2020, the Kingdom announced the establishment of a women's football league, a significant step in promoting women's sports inside the country. (The league currently includes twenty-four teams!) The government has also opened fitness centers that cater especially for women, including the Princess Reema Sports Center in Riyadh, the largest women's-only sports center in the world.

Entertainment and Public Life

While in the past women were largely excluded from the public sphere, their participation in the country's cultural scene has increased markedly in recent years. A great illustration of this is the rise of Saudi women DJs. Despite facing initial resistance and criticism from conservative elements inside the country, female DJs are now performing at major events and festivals, such as the Jeddah World Fest and the MDL Beast Festival; the women are breaking down barriers.

Moreover, there has been an increasing number of women participating in the fields of acting, singing, and modeling. Several contemporary Saudi female artists have gained popularity both in the country and internationally. For example, the singer Rotana Tarabzouni has become known for her modern take on traditional Arabian music, while the actress Fatima Al-Banawi has gained acclaim for her performances in various films and TV series. These changes, brought in under the leadership of MBS, as with those mentioned above, represent great change for the prospects of women inside the Kingdom.

In the Family and at Home

With all the changes taking place, women still have a central role at home, but with more and more entering the workforce, many now face the challenges of juggling work life and family responsibilities. There have also been many changes to the laws around family life that give women more power in the decision-making of family matters. These include the new family law mentioned earlier; between 2019 and 2021, Saudi Arabia began allowing women to register a marriage, divorce, or child's birth, and to obtain family documents such as marriage certificates without the need for consent from a male guardian.

The ability for women to obtain a divorce without the need for their husband's consent has given women greater agency in their family life and has led to a rise in divorce rates in the country. However, divorce still carries somewhat of a social stigma in Saudi Arabia and there is ongoing debate around the impact of these legal changes on family dynamics and children's upbringing. Polygamy still is legal in the Kingdom and men can have up to four wives, as long as they are able to financially support all of them and their children. For the vast majority, however, monogamy is the preference.

ATTITUDES TOWARD FOREIGNERS

Saudis have a general fondness for and curiosity about people from other countries. Their interest is genuine and the warm treatment newcomers receive is why many foreigners end up remaining in the country for longer than they'd planned to.

For Saudis, hospitality is a matter of honor and a sacred duty. One reason for this is that the Bedouin historically lived in an extremely harsh desert environment where nomads depended on each other's hospitality to survive thirst, hunger, and sudden raids or enemy attacks. Islam extends this to anyone living in Muslim lands under a "covenant" that guarantees them the protection of their hosts. Therefore, Saudis have a sense that they are charged with your welfare and safety, and they are not shy about it. A sincere and oftentimes animated welcome is what most foreigners can expect to receive in the Kingdom.

Westerners
Visitors and expatriates from the West can look forward to respectful treatment the likes of which

they may not encounter at home. Their path through the Kingdom's bureaucracy will be smoothed at every turn, and Western expats are paid generously for their contributions to Saudi society. Saudis have a particularly high regard for Americans. Crown Prince Mohammed Bin Salman went so far as to say in 2017 in a *Washington Post* interview that without America's cultural influence on Saudi Arabia, "we would have ended up like North Korea."

It is American products that Saudis seem to trust the most. The majority of their arms acquisitions come from the US, and it's common to see many American cars on the roads. The supermarket shelves have for years been stocked with American foods, which today includes those for gluten-free, vegan, and lactose-intolerant diets.

At the same time, there have also been long-held suspicions about the influence of America and American culture, both within the Kingdom and the wider Arab world. There are those who have always seen (and likely will always see) the United States as the root of all problems in the Middle East, and perhaps the world, too. These beliefs often reflect a somewhat outdated prejudice. Still, it does not prevent the widespread use of American products or the adoption of cultural trends by those who espouse these views.

Regardless of a Saudi's political opinions, they will take care to assure you that they hold no grudge against you personally. Whether your homeland is a staunch ally in America's "war on terror" or not, you can expect to be treated with courtesy. There will be curious glances but no hostility as you go about your daily life.

There are currently around eighty thousand Americans in Saudi Arabia. In the past they mainly worked for Saudi Aramco and various defense contractors like Vinnell. Nowadays, however, Americans can be found working all across the Kingdom in the Giga Projects, universities, and consultancies. Giga Project-related jobs have more recently joined Aramco and KAUST among the highest-paying jobs in the Kingdom.

Next come some thirty-thousand Britons—doctors, engineers working for British Aerospace, and the like— followed by thousands of other EU citizens dispatched by companies from their home countries.

Often these expat employees are accommodated in walled compounds, but more and more expats are ditching the compound and opting to live in apartment complexes alongside Saudis.

Most Saudis enjoy the opportunity to converse with Westerners, even if they have very limited English. Don't be surprised if they even attempt to converse with you purely in Arabic! It comes from a heartfelt sense of curiosity about people, and they are interested to know why they are in the Kingdom. Due to the importance of personal privacy and respect in Saudi culture, visitors are seldom exposed to invasive questions.

Asian Expats

Workers and laborers from Asia fulfill many essential roles in the Kingdom, predominantly in the fields of construction and industry, as well as in domestic jobs, working as nannies, drivers, and housemaids, and numerous service-related positions including in restaurants, hotels, and shops. Saudization efforts have seen more Saudis enter some of these roles, but the majority today are still filled by workers from the Philippines, Indonesia, Bangladesh, Pakistan, India, Sri Lanka, and elsewhere.

The international community has long criticized the conditions and treatment of workers in Saudi Arabia and the Gulf region, but sweeping reforms to Saudi labor law enacted in recent years have seen conditions vastly improve. For example, employers are no longer allowed to retain the passports of their employees and so workers can now more easily change jobs at their own will. Foreign workers also no longer need to obtain an NOC (No Objection Certificate)—a document from their employer that states they may leave their job to obtain another.

Workers are now limited to working eight hours a day for a maximum of six days a week. Those that work above that are entitled to an overtime rate that is 50 percent higher than their regular wage. The government has also banned working outside in the sun from 12:00 to 3:00 p.m. from June 15 to September 15, when temperatures are at their highest.

Non-Muslims in a Muslim Society
Non-Muslims are forbidden from entering the holy cities of Mecca and Medina. It would not be wise to try and disobey this rule; those caught risk a hefty fine and deportation. The boundary is a 30-mile (48-km) radius

around the holy cities, and road signs on the approach from Jeddah make it clear where to turn off. Saudi Arabia also bans non-Muslims from entering mosques throughout the country, so sightseeing is limited to the exterior.

Many expats have wondered whether they can celebrate their country's traditional or religious holidays while in Saudi Arabia. With Islam being the sole national religion, it has long been the rule that publicly practicing other religions or celebrating their festivals are forbidden. What you do in the privacy of your own home, however, is largely up to you. Officially, any observation of your own traditions or religion is permitted if it is limited to your own home and not advertised in any way. Establishing a public meeting place or attempting to convert people are strictly forbidden. Bringing a Bible or other religious book is acceptable as long as it is a single copy intended for personal use. With that said, more and more celebrations of Western traditions and holidays are popping up all over. Recent years have seen Halloween celebrations with costumes in Saudi Arabia, and it's now common to find non-religious Christmas and Easter decorations for sale in shopping malls.

Visitors and expats working in the Kingdom should take care to adopt a cordial and respectful attitude when conversing with Saudis. While there's no harm in showing some of your personality, it would be in bad taste to talk about things like parties and drinking, boyfriends or girlfriends, or anything else that may offend their cultural norms and religious values. Keep in

CULTURAL SENSITIVITY WHEN INTERACTING WITH YOUR MUSLIM FRIENDS AND COLLEAGUES? YES!

In addition to being familiar with local norms, it's important to understand which topics are best avoided or approached with sensitivity. When visiting Saudi, people will often talk to you about Islam. In Western countries, if people talk to us about religion, we may say something like "Listen, thanks, but I'm not interested." However, in Saudi this would be considered insensitive and akin to saying that you're not interested in hearing about a subject of great importance to the person you are talking to. Simply put, Saudis are deeply proud of their religion and so it's advisable to participate in conversations about Islam. In learning about their culture and traditions, you will also gain insight into what's most important to them. When Saudis talk about Islam you needn't assume that they are trying to convert you (or "revert" you, as the process is referred to in Islam). They are equally happy for the opportunity to discuss Islam with you and to educate you about it.

Care should also be taken regarding the name Mohammed. Keeping in mind that Prophet Mohammed is the central figure in Islam, it would be inappropriate to misuse the name.

Regarding topics to avoid, one key topic is the friction between Sunnis and Shias. It is a sensitive topic that foreigners and non-Muslims often struggle to fully grasp. By the same token, it is advisable to avoid talking about political issues like the war in Yemen, or the country's relationship with Israel.

One final issue that a lot of visitors inadvertently run into is how to respond to the ubiquitous "*Insha'Allah*." The phrase, often shortened to *Inshallah*, means "God willing" and is central to the Islamic and, by extension, Saudi belief system. You'll hear it after nearly every kind of statement of intent, promise, or commitment. Since visitors are not usually accustomed to hearing mundane actions deferred to the will of God, they sometimes fall into the trap of making a sarcastic remark in response.

For example:

"*See you tomorrow, teacher.*"

"*See you tomorrow. Please bring your completed homework with you.*"

"*Inshallah.*"

"(Scoffs) *Ha! Does that mean you're really going to bring it this time?*"

Depending on the familiarity of the two speakers, this kind of response may be interpreted as insensitive. Saudis are extremely courteous, though, and so will probably never make a point of saying as much. Relationships will benefit if remarks such as these are avoided. A simple smile or saying "*Inshallah*" in response will suffice in most circumstances.

mind, too, that dating, i.e., mixing and intimacy between two people who are unmarried, is illegal and considered immoral. For more on this topic, see Chapter 4.

EDUCATION AND WORK

In 2023, the literacy rate in Saudi Arabia was 96.3 percent. In the Kingdom's early years, education was offered in a handful of *madrasas*, or Islamic schools, and the rest was up to individual parents. Now, parents can choose between sending their children to public, private, or international schools.

All schools are regulated by the Ministry of Education and the General Presidency of Girls' Education. Saudi government schools are reserved for Saudi citizens; non-resident children who are Muslim can also enroll here. These schools are separated by gender, and Islamic studies is a large focus of their education. Primary schools run by the government are free and available to all Saudi citizens. There are also private schools that follow the national curriculum and teach in either Arabic or English, or a mix of both languages. Students attend primary school between the ages of six and twelve, and it's compulsory for both boys and girls to attend all six years. Education beyond the age of twelve, however, is not compulsory.

After elementary school, there is normally a split into intermediate and secondary stages, for students aged thirteen to sixteen and seventeen and nineteen, respectively. Both intermediary and secondary school are free for Saudis and include a curriculum of Islamic studies, Arabic, history, math, literature, science, and in many schools, English. Beyond completion of intermediate school, students can choose a secondary school with a particular focus on subjects including sciences, business, or arts. Before graduating, students in government schools take the GAT (General Aptitude Test), which is required by most Saudi universities for admission.

With so many foreign expats in the Kingdom, there are many schools that cater for children from specific countries. They use the relevant language for instruction and examination system, as well as those that offer the International Baccalaureate. Costs for international schools can be expensive and vary from approximately 15,000 SAR to 100,000 SAR per year.

When it comes to higher education, there are now twenty-five public universities in the country, nine private universities, and thirty-four private colleges. The number of higher education centers continues to grow along with increasing demand, and numerous foreign universities have established campuses in Saudi Arabia, too. The majority of the Saudi student body at university level is female, who made up approximately 52 percent of the students in 2024.

The Saudi government popularly sponsors students to study abroad through the Custodian of the Two Holy Mosques Scholarship Program. By way of a snapshot, in 2018 the program sponsored 114,000 students. The most popular destinations were USA, the UK, Canada, Australia, and Germany.

CHAPTER THREE

CUSTOMS & TRADITIONS

CALENDARS

The Saudi year is measured by the Muslim lunar calendar from the birth of Islam. Thus 2024 is 1445/46 *hijri* (after Mohammed's emigration from Mecca to Medina), the lunar year having about 354 days—there is a prohibition on intercalary or leap months in the Qur'an. Newspapers list both *hijri* and CE, while banks and other big businesses tend to use the Gregorian calendar for convenience. Civic holidays such as National Day are also marked using the Gregorian calendar.

The workweek in Saudi Arabia is Sunday to Thursday. Friday and Saturday form the weekend, while Friday is especially reserved for prayer.

RAMADAN

The month of Ramadan, the ninth month of the Islamic calendar during which the Qur'an was revealed, is

Men gather to break the day's fast at Masjid al-Haram in Mecca during the month of Ramadan.

dedicated to the duty of fasting, to prayers, and to charity. All able-bodied adults must fast from sunrise to sunset for thirty days—that means no food, water, coffee, cigarettes, or even chewing gum during daylight hours. People who are unwell, menstruating women, and travelers are excused from fasting. Sex is also forbidden from dawn to dusk.

The month begins with the sighting of the new moon, which must be sighted by several witnesses, rather than calculated by astronomical means, for Ramadan to start and end. This means that the dates for Ramadan can vary slightly from country to country. Once the start of Ramadan has been declared, people wish each other a "*Ramadan kareem*" or "*Ramadan mubarak.*"

At sunset, the fast is broken with the *iftar* meal, which traditionally consists of a handful of dates and a drink of water or juice. The wealthy set up long *iftar* tables on their property, and everyone is welcome to eat. Restaurants will include special dishes and a variety of delicious additions to the menu during Ramadan. Take care when driving close to *iftar* time, as you will find many people in a rush. In practice, the feast continues throughout the night as people nibble on special Ramadan treats such as date cakes, or *kalaj*, a pastry of thin sheets of dough dipped in milk, stuffed with a heavy cream, deep-fried, and sprinkled with sugar or drizzled with honey. It's common to see people selling home-cooked food in specially erected tents along the streets and in parks; these popular traditional treats are created according to homemade recipes and are well worth sampling.

Some people sleep through the daylight hours during Ramadan. Schedules flip and night turns into day: the streets and mosques are lit up with festive decorations— the writing with light, or *mahya*—and teeming with people. Shops, malls, and restaurants stay open until late, and it's common for people to catch up on work during the evenings or into the night. Those working in the

Maamoul, buttermilk cookies filled with dried dates or figs, are a popular post-fast treat.

Kingdom shouldn't be surprised to receive work-related messages, phone calls, or emails late at night over the course of the month.

Generally speaking, however, it's business as usual during Ramadan, with a few caveats. Most workplaces observe a reduced schedule; depending on the company, Muslims may work from 10:00 a.m. to 4:00 p.m. or midday to 6:00 p.m., while non-Muslim expats will most often continue to work a normal schedule.

Productivity at work may slow down during this period, but it's rare to encounter Saudis who expect to be excused from their duties just because it's Ramadan. Most will carry on as if it's any normal day, and even though they have been without water, coffee, and food since waking up, it's often barely noticeable. People will be as helpful and pleasant as always.

If you are working in the Kingdom or visiting for any length of time, you will invariably receive a few *iftar* meal invitations, and this is an experience you don't want to miss. Your hosts will pull out all the stops and the food will be delicious.

The last ten days are the most important of the whole month. People begin to plan the Eid festivities and expectations build toward Laylatul Qadr (Night of Decree or the Night of Power). It is one of the most sacred nights in the Islamic calendar and represents the night that the Qur'an was revealed to Prophet Muhammed. On this night, the pious engage in extended nighttime prayers (Qiyam-ul-Layl) through the night, read the Qur'an, or recite specific verses that hold special meaning for them, seeking Allah's mercy, blessings, and forgiveness.

It's believed that prayers made on this night are more efficacious than those made during the rest of the year.

At the sighting of the new moon, Ramadan culminates in the holiday of Eid al-Fitr. From that point it is customary for people to wish each other "*Eid mubarak!*" The holiday officially lasts for three days, but it normally becomes a whole week at most Saudi workplaces. For more on Eid, see page 86.

It should be noted that the dates of Ramadan are not fixed. As Ramadan is based on the lunar Hijri calendar, the dates shift about ten to twelve days earlier every year on the Gregorian calendar.

POINTS OF ETIQUETTE

Whether a short-term visitor or a working expat during the month of Ramadan, ethical conduct and a calm demeanor are paramount.

- If in normal times it's inadvisable to show frustration or anger, during Ramadan, a month dedicated to reflection and prayer, it's all the more important to remain composed and friendly at all times. If you are working, you can show support for your colleagues, as well as flexibility with schedule changes. If you are a manager, consider hosting a team or company *iftar*.
- At home, take care not to play music loudly, shout, or disturb the peace during this time.

- Those working should take care not to eat, drink, chew gum, or smoke in front of colleagues who are fasting. This includes taking sips from your water bottle or munching on snacks while at your desk. All consumables should be placed inside a drawer, out of sight, even though most Saudis are extremely understanding and will tell you, "Go ahead, it's okay!" In most workplaces, there will be a designated Ramadan kitchen or other room with a closed door, where you can have your coffee, tea, or lunch out of sight of those who are fasting.

- When out and about, restaurants and shops will only open after sundown. It's often possible to find a single restaurant open in any given area, mainly for construction workers; however, it can be tricky to locate as they will often have the blinds down and the lights off!

- Modest dress should be diligently followed during this month. This means covering arms, shoulders, torso and midriff, legs, and not wearing anything too tight or revealing.

- Ramadan is a good opportunity to connect with people, to indulge in delicious *iftar* meals at sundown where you can learn about different types of food, and delight in the company of new friends or acquaintances. Join in the public festivities and you will find the experience to be a very positive one.

Pilgrims circle the Kaaba seven times as part of the *tawaf* ritual.

THE HAJJ

During the lunar month of Dhul-Hijjah, millions of
Muslims make their way to the Kingdom to perform the
rituals of pilgrimage. As the Qur'an instructs, pilgrims
must embark on Hajj in a state of physical purity called
ihram, which means wearing all white, and not applying
any lotions, creams, or perfumes to the skin from the
moment they set off. Don't be surprised if, traveling to
Saudi Arabia during this month, many of your fellow
passengers will be dressed this way.

As we have seen, the origins of the pilgrimage go back
to pre-Islamic times, but it was fully assimilated as the
central event of the Islamic year. The Qur'an tells every
able-bodied Muslim to perform the Hajj at least once
in a lifetime, and for many it is a lifelong ambition.

Pilgrims follow in the footsteps of the Prophet Mohammed: the sacred sites along the pilgrimage route formed the backdrop to the most important events of his life. Pilgrims spend a night in prayer near the town of Mina, which turns into an enormous tent city. On the morning of the following day, they proceed to the Plain of Arafat, where they perform Wuquf, the central ritual of the Hajj, the standing prayer, from noon to sunset.

Back in Mecca, the rituals include the *tawaf*, which consists of walking counterclockwise seven times around the Kaaba. This is a cuboid structure at the center of the Grand Mosque roughly facing the four points of the compass, which contains a black stone believed to be a meteorite fragment and is covered with a black silk cloth. According to the Qur'an, the structure was built by Ibrahim (Abraham) and his son Ismail (Ishmael). The Prophet, when he established Islam, cleared it of the pagan idols the Meccans had housed there. All Muslims, wherever they are in the world, face the Kaaba when they pray.

Another ritual in the Grand Mosque compound is the *sa'i*, walking seven times back and forth between the hills of Safa and Marwah—a reenactment of the search of Hagar, Ibrahim's wife, for water for Ismail before the Zamzam well there was revealed to her. Many pilgrims also drink from the well.

Managing the Pilgrimage

Marshaling these huge numbers of pilgrims is one of the Kingdom's great logistical achievements. While accidents do occur—a particularly dangerous spot for stampedes is

Jamrat, a pillar representing the devil and ritually stoned by pilgrims. Tragically, in 2015, some two-thousand pilgrims died while performing Hajj as a result of a stampede and overcrowding.

There is a government minister solely responsible for Hajj affairs, who allots annual quotas to Muslim countries for the number of pilgrims they may send. Airport buildings, roads, water, and health facilities are provided for pilgrims, notably the tented Hajj terminal at King Abdul Aziz Airport in Jeddah. The government also distributes bottled water, juice, and boxed lunches during the climbing of Mount Arafat and stations ambulances in strategic locations. Private vendors also come to sell tea and snacks, while others provide refreshments for free on the streets to pilgrims.

The government also relieves pilgrims of the task of having to slaughter a sacrificial beast. The Islamic Development Bank now sells coupons for animals, which are chosen by the pilgrim and then slaughtered, processed, and frozen for distribution among the poor, first in Mecca and then throughout the rest of the Muslim world.

The Hajj is an important source of income for the Hijaz. Many pilgrims will also do some shopping for electronics and textiles in Jeddah, for centuries the port of entry and traditionally reliant on the Hajj and Umrah (or lesser pilgrimage) for its economy. In the old days, the local emir used to exact exorbitant taxes on pilgrims in return for his "protection." Jeddah's textile traders say they essentially do a year's business during the month.

UMRAH

Umrah, on the other hand, is a smaller pilgrimage that can be performed at any time of the year. It involves fewer rituals than Hajj, and it is not mandatory for Muslims to perform it. There are five rituals in Umrah starting with Niyyah, which means intention—a declaration affirming that you want to start your Umrah. Then comes Ihram, Tawaf, and Sa'i. At the end, pilgrims must cut their hair. Men can either get their hair trimmed, called *taqseer*, or shave the whole head, called *haleq*. Women pilgrims normally do the *taqseer*.

NATIONAL HOLIDAYS

Eid al-Fitr

This three-day festival signifying the breaking of the fast falls on the new moon at the end of Ramadan; the date depends on the sighting of the new moon with the naked eye around sunset.

When Eid al-Fitr comes, everyone puts on their best clothes. Before a short communal prayer in the early morning every Muslim must pay *zakat*, or alms, donating food for the poor or a cash equivalent that is collected at mosques. Those who can give generously at this time of year. The prayer is followed by a sermon. The faithful exchange hugs to a cry of "*Eid mubarak*," and then feast and visit relatives and friends. In addition to the many hugs, kisses, and visits to friends and family, Saudis will send hundreds of text messages with Eid wishes.

Dancers perform as part of Eid al-Fitr celebrations.

It's common for Saudis to travel abroad during Eid holidays. In the week or so following Ramadan, shops tend to close, and the streets can seem quieter than usual.

Eid al-Adha

Again a three-day holiday, Eid al-Adha falls roughly seventy days after Eid al-Fitr and marks the end of the official Hajj season, when pilgrims descend from Mount Arafat. Men, women, and children again dress in their best clothes and perform the Eid prayer. Muslims who can afford it slaughter their best livestock, if they own any—usually sheep but also camels, cows, and goats—or buy an animal for the purpose. Slaughter is carried out according to strict ritual (*dhabiha*) and is meant to cause the least suffering possible to the animal. Since the animal is traditionally bled out, this can be a rather gory affair for some Western sensibilities. The event celebrates Ibrahim's willingness to sacrifice his son Ishmael at Marwah (Abraham and Isaac at Mount Moriah in the Jewish tradition). The meat is divided up into three parts: one-third is kept for the immediate family, a third is for the community (extended family and neighbors), and a third is donated to the poor.

Saudi National Day: September 23

This falls on the Gregorian date of September 23 and marks the Kingdom's foundation in 1932. The day commemorates the declaration of Saudi Arabia's unification by King Abdulaziz bin Abdul Rahman Al-Faisal Al Saud. During National Day there are green Saudi flags everywhere, and large outdoor festivals with family activities, entertainment, music, and food for all to enjoy. If Saudi National Day falls on a weekday, it is taken as a public holiday, and often the king will declare one extra day before or after National Day as an additional off day.

Founding Day: February 22

A royal decree issued by King Salman in 2022 named a new annual holiday on this day to commemorate the day Imam Muhammad bin Saud established the first Saudi state in 1727 CE/ 1139 AH when he was enthroned as the emir of Diriyah. It is a public holiday

and in 2023 was commemorated with a military
air show and events that spotlighted the country's
cultural heritage.

Flag Day: March 11

First observed in 2023 and another new annual
national holiday, Flag Day is celebrated on March 11
to commemorate the day when the Saudi national
flag was adopted by Ibn Saud in 1937.

SEASON'S GREETINGS

Many young Saudis have now adopted Western
celebrations like Valentine's Day, Halloween, and even
Christmas (though not its religious aspects). This is
largely due to globalization and the influence of social
media. In the past, if expat families wanted to celebrate
religious holidays, they could do so privately in their
homes or compounds. Nowadays, it's becoming more
common to see evidence of these holidays out in the
open, such as via the display of novelty items for sale
in shopping malls and superstores.

Where there are public festive displays, for example,
around Christmas, you will find it is the non-religious
features of Christmas that are displayed, without
religious significance. For example, you may see
Christmas trees, candy canes, and stockings on display,
but not nativity scenes. The same is also true for Easter:
you may find bunny rabbit figurines and chocolate
eggs for sale, but you won't find wooden crosses.

Trends of Tolerance

In 2023, when Easter Sunday coincided with Ramadan, much to everyone's surprise, there were several Easter dinners combined with *iftar* meals held around Riyadh, with chocolate bunny rabbits and colored eggs used as decorations and gifts.

In April 2023, the front page of English-language daily *Arab News* featured a "Spotlight on Easter," which discussed Easter traditions in the United States and how American expats and their families were celebrating their Easter while in Saudi.

SUPERSTITION

Superstition and traditional beliefs are quite common in Saudi Arabia, as they are in much of the world. These beliefs can vary quite widely from region to region. It's also worth mentioning that while these beliefs are commonly found, they are not necessarily held by everyone, and particularly those that do not have a religious source. Here are just a few examples of traditional beliefs that you will come across.

As in much of the Middle East, there is a fear of the "evil eye." Aroused by envy and jealousy, it is believed that it causes harm or misfortune, especially to young children and babies. As a result, people use amulets and talismans to ward it off, attaching them to their cars or shop windows. These may be in the shape of a single eye, the likes of which you will often find painted on the back of trucks, or little Quranic scrolls that dangle from the rearview mirror or sit in display windows. Saying "*Mashallah*" (praise be to God) is also believed to fend off the evil eye and is therefore used when congratulating someone on good luck or an achievement.

Many people believe that black cats are a symbol of bad luck, and some people believe that they bring misfortune or disease. This belief may stem from Islamic traditions that associate black cats with the devil or *jinn* (malevolent spirits).

Certain numbers are considered unlucky in Saudi Arabia, such as the number 13. As a result, some people may avoid using or doing things in multiples of these numbers, such as avoiding sitting at a table with 13 people, and it's not unusual to see tall buildings with no thirteenth floor! Friday 13 is also considered an unlucky day in Saudi Arabia, and some people may avoid making important decisions or taking risks on that day.

Many in Saudi believe dreams to hold symbolic and even prophetic meaning, and some people may consult dream interpreters to try to understand what's being communicated.

Before embarking on a task, from starting their car to sitting down to a meal, people invoke divine protection by muttering the first word of the Qur'an, "*Bismillah*"—in the name of God. Belief in *kismet* (fate) is very strong, to the point where Arabs seem quite fatalistic: everything is ordained and will happen *inshallah*, if God wills it. Still, one popular proverb declares, "Trust the Lord, but tether your camel!"

RITES OF PASSAGE

Birth

In Saudi Arabia, the birth of a child is a significant event in a family's life. As we've seen, the culture of Saudi Arabia places strong emphasis on family values, and the arrival of a new baby is an occasion to celebrate and carry out several rites of passage. These practices are largely influenced by Islamic customs and teachings, aiming to ensure the spiritual well-being of the child and the family.

One of the first rites of passage after a child is born is the recitation of the Adhan, the Islamic call to prayer. The father or a close male family member gently whispers the Adhan into the baby's right ear, signifying the introduction of the child to the Islamic faith. This practice is believed to be a form of spiritual protection and guidance for the newborn.

Aqiqah Ceremony

Typically held on the seventh day after birth, the Aqiqah ceremony is a significant rite of passage in Saudi Arabia. The family slaughters one or two animals (usually sheep or goats) as a sacrifice and distributes the meat among relatives, friends, and the less fortunate. This act of giving is considered a form of gratitude to Allah for the gift of a child and also serves as a means to share their joy with the community.

As part of the Aqiqah ceremony, it's customary in Saudi Arabia to shave the newborn's head. This ritual symbolizes the cleansing of the baby from impurities and is believed to promote healthy hair growth. The weight of the shaved hair is often measured, and an equivalent amount of money or gold is donated to charity as another act of gratitude and giving back to the community.

Naming the child is an important aspect of Saudi culture. In accordance with Islamic tradition, parents in Saudi Arabia choose a name with a positive meaning, often inspired by Islamic history or the names of Prophets, companions, or other significant religious figures. The chosen name is announced during the Aqiqah ceremony.

Welcoming the Newborn

Family and friends visit the new parents to offer congratulations and blessings. It is customary for visitors to bring gifts for the baby, such as clothing, toys, or gold jewelry. These visits help to strengthen family bonds and provide emotional support to the new parents.

Circumcision

Circumcision plays a significant role in the rites of passage for young boys in Saudi Arabia. This procedure, known as "*khitan*" in Arabic, is deeply rooted in religious, cultural, and social traditions.

Religious Significance

Circumcision is a religious duty that is believed to date back to Prophet Ibrahim (Abraham) who was commanded by God to circumcise his son, Isma'il (Ishmael). It is considered an essential aspect of Islamic faith—as it is in Judaism—and is prescribed by the Hadith (sayings and actions of Prophet Muhammad).

Age and Timing

In the past, the age of circumcision varied depending on family preferences, regional customs, and the child's health. Today, most families perform the procedure within the first four weeks of birth. Traditionally, circumcision was carried out by a skilled elder or religious figure in the community. Nowadays it is typically carried out by a medical professional in a hospital, using local anesthesia.

Birthdays

Though not unheard of, birthdays have not traditionally been celebrated in Saudi Arabia. Many conventional Saudi families believed that only two Eids (Eid al-Fitr and Eid al-Adha) should be celebrated, as these are the only festivals mentioned in Islamic teachings. Among older generations, unified birthday celebrations were sometimes held on Eid holidays. Today, however, birthday celebrations are becoming more common. Globalization, the influence of social media, an increasing number of Saudis traveling abroad, and an increasing number of foreigners visiting that country have all played their part in this shift in cultural norms. For the younger generation, it is being embraced as a means to express individuality and to build stronger social connections.

When they are celebrated, birthdays in Saudi Arabia are intimate affairs, with family members gathering at home to share a meal and spend time together. The person whose birthday it is will be showered with blessings and well wishes, and sometimes small gifts are exchanged.

For those who organize more elaborate affairs, there will be a party with music, dancing, and a variety of food, and of course a birthday cake. As birthday celebrations grow in popularity, they have been adapted to suit Saudi customs and traditions. For instance, traditional foods like *kabsa* (a rice dish) and desserts like *umm Ali* (a bread pudding) will often be served.

Popular themes for children's parties include superheroes, princesses, and cartoon characters. Teenagers and adults may opt for more sophisticated themes or focus on a specific color scheme or design.

Graduation

Graduation is a significant rite of passage in Saudi today that symbolizes the beginning of a new stage in the young person's life. Education holds great importance in the Kingdom, with the government heavily investing in the sector to ensure the development of a skilled workforce and promote social progress. As such, graduation is seen not only as an achievement for the individual but also as a contribution to the nation's growth and prosperity.

Graduation ceremonies are a fusion of traditional customs and modern practices, reflecting the country's deep-rooted cultural values and its progressive outlook. The ceremony often begins with the recitation of verses from the Qur'an, seeking blessings and guidance from Allah for the graduating students as they embark on their new journey.

Professors and graduates, dressed in traditional academic regalia, enter the venue in a procession, signifying the importance and formality of the occasion.

Students are awarded their diplomas or degrees, symbolizing the culmination of their academic journey. Awards and honors may also be presented to students who have excelled in their studies or made outstanding contributions to their academic community. Prominent figures, such as university faculty, alumni, or public figures, deliver speeches to inspire and motivate the graduating students, offering wisdom and advice for their future endeavors.

Traditional Saudi music and dance performances may be included in the ceremony, adding a festive atmosphere to the event.

Graduation is a time for families to come together and celebrate their loved one's achievements. It is customary for families to host a gathering at their home or a banquet hall, inviting relatives and friends to join in the festivities. Traditional Saudi cuisine is served, and guests often bring gifts to congratulate the graduate. Gifts may include gold or silver jewelry, electronic gadgets, or even cash, depending on the preferences of the graduate and the financial means of the giver.

Graduates and their families have always dressed up for the occasion, with men and women both in traditional formal clothes. Nowadays, customized dresses with intricately designed caps and gowns have become more common.

Weddings

In Saudi Arabia, weddings are grand and meticulously organized events that celebrate the union of a man and

Celebrants dance at a wedding ceremony.

a woman plus their families. The cultural customs and traditions associated with marriage ceremonies in the country are quite exceptional and deeply rooted. The diversity in traditions across various regions of Saudi Arabia is notable, too. Saudi weddings typically have an extensive guest list, with attendance sometimes reaching several hundred people. Attending a Saudi wedding can be a unique experience, and it is essential to understand what one might expect.

Firstly, it is customary for marriages to be arranged, with the responsibility of finding a suitable bride falling on the groom's family. The traditional process involves the groom approaching the bride's father or eldest male relative to request her hand in marriage. The families then evaluate the couple's compatibility based on criteria such as education, financial stability, social status, and family background. If the bride's father or guardian approves, the families proceed to read the Surat Al-Fatiha, the first chapter of the Qur'an, to mark the beginning of the union.

Following the proposal, a senior female member of the groom's family informs the mother of the prospective bride about the groom's intention to marry her daughter. If both families agree to the match, the bride is then invited to formally unveil herself in the presence of her future husband.

How Do Arranged Marriages Work In Modern Saudi Society?

According to a Saudi female friend, in many cases the woman will already know the person, for example, from work, or places where people go to socialize. If a man wants to marry a girl, she will give the phone number of a family member for the man's family to call and discuss the possibility of marriage. "We might know the person," she says "but we don't show it, especially in conservative families." If both families agree to the union, they will proceed with the engagement.

An engagement ceremony, known as *al-khitbah* will take place. During this ceremony, the families will gather to celebrate and exchange gifts. The groom will give the bride a *mahr* (dowry), a requirement coming from the Qur'an. The type of gift or amount of money given differs between families, regions, and tribes. For many it is a financial gift given by the groom to the bride, and other times it may be gold, or even property. Some families give a high amount in order to show the best of themselves. It's also common nowadays for couples to agree on a symbolic or nominal amount, reflecting a modern shift away from traditional dowry practices.

The betrothed then exchange rings, each placing a ring onto the index finger of the other's right hand. The *makhtubayn*, also known as betrothal, involves a gathering of the families of the bride and groom to determine the schedule of wedding-related events. The purpose of this meeting is to formally agree on the dates of each occasion and make public announcements accordingly.

Following the engagement, the couple will enter into a marriage contract known as *aqd al-Nikah*. These serve as both the official marriage ceremony and the registration of the union, taking place concurrently with the dowry agreement. During this event, the imam delivers a brief speech emphasizing the importance of honoring one's spouse and discussing the religious aspects of marriage. Subsequently, the couple completes and signs the legal documents, which are also witnessed, signifying the official marriage of the pair. Traditionally, this ceremony occurs in either the bride or groom's home, but it can also be held at a mosque or a courthouse.

Ghumra, also known as the henna party, is a traditional pre-wedding celebration for the bride and women in her family, as well as her friends. This centuries-old custom used to be an intimate gathering, but nowadays it has become an elaborate event that is almost like a bachelorette party. It is celebrated in beautifully decorated venues with music and stunning outfits.

The party usually takes place on the night before the wedding, and the bride's female relatives and friends come together to enjoy food, music (played by female musicians), and dancing. One of the highlights of the *ghumra* is the application of henna, in which a female henna artist decorates the palms and feet of the bride and her guests.

The groom also has his own celebration in which his face is shaved by a close male friend or family member. His male relatives and friends then dance to traditional music before he visits the bride. During this visit, he presents the *mahr* (dowry).

Whether the *ghumra* is traditional or modern, the bride always dresses in the *itthyab*, which is an elaborately embroidered traditional gown. Meanwhile, the groom wears a traditional *thobe.*

Saudi Arabian wedding ceremonies are known for their opulence and grandeur, often taking place in lavishly decorated ballrooms or luxurious hotels. These events typically begin late in the evening, around 10:00 p.m., with the bride making her entrance close to midnight.

As the celebration commences, men and women gather in separate halls filled with tables overflowing with food and beverages. Live bands play music while guests dance the night away, sometimes until the early hours.

The bride and groom take their seats at the head of the reception, akin to a king and queen, and are honored by a toast to their health. One of the key moments of the ceremony is when the couple switches their engagement rings from their right index fingers to their left ring fingers, symbolizing their new marital status.

Following the ring exchange, the festivities truly kick off. In contemporary Saudi Arabian weddings, the bride and groom share a first dance together. Afterward, guests join in on the dancing, with men and women dancing separately within the reception hall.

While women celebrate and dance in a nearby ballroom, men participate in a traditional dance called *ardah*. How the dance is performed differs from one region to another. It can be done with two rows of men standing shoulder to shoulder facing each other, holding long, thin swords, and moving to the beat of drums and chanted poetry. The rhythm of the drums dictates the men to raise and lower their swords. *Ardah* dance has a rich history in Saudi culture and was once performed to boost the morale of warriors before a battle. Today, it is performed at various ceremonies, including religious holidays, births, and graduations.

When it comes to attire, brides often opt for a white, Western-style wedding gown, complete with intricate lace detailing. Meanwhile, grooms typically don a white *thobe*—the traditional long-sleeved, ankle-length robe. This is paired with a black *bisht*, a lengthy cloak adorned with golden accents. It's worth noting that *bishts* are reserved for special occasions and festivals, as well as being worn by royalty and the elderly.

Weddings are celebrated with a grand feast known as *walimah*. This feast is characterized by its extravagant spread of food and drinks, where no one goes hungry. The main course of the *walimah* feast often features a baby camel or a whole roasted sheep, which are considered delicacies and only served on special occasions. These dishes stem from tribal traditions and are usually served with rice and flatbread. Additionally, a wide variety of salads and side dishes are available to guests, all presented buffet style. To quench their thirst, guests can enjoy free-flowing fruit mocktails and traditional Arabic coffee. The dessert section includes delectable dates, pastries, and chocolates that guests can indulge in.

Funerals

In line with Islamic custom, someone who passes away is usually buried within twenty-four hours, as that is believed to give respect to the deceased. In some circumstances, families may keep the dead body for longer while waiting for relatives from other cities to arrive and pay their respects. Upon the death of an individual, the family and close friends gather around the deceased to recite prayers and offer condolences. The deceased person's eyes are closed, and the body is covered with a clean sheet. It's customary to recite the *Shahada,* the declaration of faith in Islam, as the soul is believed to leave the body at this time. These events are segregated by gender, with women offering condolences in one section of the house and men in another.

The body of the deceased is then prepared for burial according to Islamic customs. This involves performing the *ghusl,* a ritual washing of the body. For a woman, this will be done only by a woman or her husband. For a man, this will be done by men. It can be done by close family members, or a person responsible for the washing at the mosque, usually a volunteer.

After washing, the body is shrouded in a plain white cloth known as the *kafan*. The shrouding process is also guided by Islamic principles, with the deceased's head wrapped separately from the body.

The funeral prayers, or *salat al-janazah*, are an essential part of the funeral. The prayers are performed in congregation, usually at the local mosque. Men and women participate in the prayers, segregated. The prayer is led by an imam, who recites verses from the Qur'an and offers supplications for the deceased.

Following the funeral prayers, the body is transported to the cemetery in a funeral procession. The procession is usually conducted on foot, with the body carried on a platform by close male relatives or friends. It is considered an honor to be chosen as a pallbearer. As the procession moves toward the cemetery, mourners recite prayers and verses from the Qur'an. Traditionally women do not take part in the burial; it is a men's only ritual.

The grave is oriented in a way that the deceased's face is turned toward the Kaaba in Mecca. The body is placed in the grave on its right side, without a coffin, and is covered with a layer of wood or stones to separate it from the soil. The grave is then filled with earth, and a simple, unadorned headstone is placed at the head of the grave to mark the burial site.

After the burial, the family of the deceased observes a mourning period called the *'iddah*. For widows, this period lasts four months and ten days, during which they refrain from wearing decorative clothing, jewelry, or makeup. For other family members, the mourning period typically lasts three days. During this time, friends and extended family members visit the grieving family to offer condolences and share in their sorrow.

CHAPTER FOUR

MAKING FRIENDS

Beyond family bonds, friendship is the most important tie that binds Saudis. Major friendships start in school, and many last a lifetime. Since Saudis attend segregated schools, friendships can develop with same-gender friends which become intense and exclusive. With changing social norms, cross-gender friendships are becoming more common, especially among younger Saudis in urban areas. And since families hold great importance, friendships also develop within extended family networks. It's also common for friends to call each other "sister" and "brother," indicating closeness and affection. When friends get married and start families, friendships may drift apart as priorities in life change.

The friendships Saudis form later in life are often in the nature of patron–client relationships and among career-oriented Saudis, it's common for friendships to take the form of a mentor–protégé relationship across different generations.

Many Saudis are open to establishing friendships with Westerners. These may take time to build, and the best approach is often simply to wait with a welcoming demeanor and let them come to you. The old adage and favorite saying of Saudis still rings true: "Patience is a virtue."

Once a friendship has been built, it is difficult to undo and can survive disappointments and betrayals that would swiftly end a friendship in the West. It's one of the great puzzles of Saudi Arabia that a wrong you have done a friend (or had done to you) will simply be forgotten. After an appropriate interval for sulking, you can suddenly find yourself embraced and forgiven as if nothing had happened.

Loyalty to friends is observed in deed more than in word, and longevity in friendships is valued and cherished. An established friendship will almost always take precedence over a new acquaintanceship or mere business ties.

MEETING SAUDIS

Saudis are curious about foreigners and the outgoing ones may approach you in public and ask you where you are from. The conversation may end with them saying "Welcome to Saudi," with a smile. The outgoing ones, or those who have been educated or done business abroad, may be happy to linger for a chat and, if at work, may strike up an easy acquaintanceship or friendship. How far this develops depends partly on you, just as it would at home. New friendships among adult Saudis are often patron–client relationships—where the person with the higher status, greater age, or more money looks after the other in return for loyalty—so expatriates may also find themselves adopted by their boss if there is a mutual liking.

When meeting across genders, Western men should be sensitive as Saudi women can be very conservative. Be careful to avoid touching, even accidentally, or as a gesture of kindness or gratitude. For example, a gentle hand on the shoulder to say thank you would not be welcomed. Western women will find Saudi men very respectful. Many women have said they feel safer in the Kingdom than in their home countries due to the level of respect from men and personal space that is kept between people of different genders. While you might get curious or friendly glances, it's very rare to find men staring outright, or looking at women's bodies, as it's considered extremely impolite and against their cultural notion of a woman's honor.

In parts of the country that see few Westerners, local dignitaries may still feel that they are charged with a guest's welfare and may welcome him as it were on behalf of the town, and even invite him to their home so he is safely looked after during his stay.

Saudis are painfully aware of the fact that, in the past, many foreigners came to Saudi only to earn money, fill up their bank accounts, and then leave. Few expats were genuinely interested in engaging with Saudi culture. Of course, nowadays the situation is very different; the lifting of restrictions has led to easier engagement with Saudi society. In any case, whatever your motives are for coming to Saudi, it would be wise not to talk about money too much and, if you're trying to do business, giving back to Saudi society in some way— perhaps by volunteering in your community or mentoring young people—will open you to many new experiences.

It's true that Saudis are easily won over, but if you really want to win their hearts, show an interest in their culture. Your efforts will be rewarded many times over.

GREETINGS

Saudis typically ask anyone they greet "How are you?" three times, and with three variations, for example, "How are you doing?", "How's everything?" Saudis will wait for your reply, and ask again. It's a very comforting experience, particularly for those who are far away from home. Quite different from the typical Western "How are you?" without a reply being expected. Men and women alike will call you "sister" or "brother," ask you how you feel in their country, and insist that you call them if you ever need help.

Saudi men are great shakers of hands and will expect to shake hands, firmly, at every meeting and parting. More traditional Saudis will then place their hand over their heart, and it would be polite for visitors to do the same. Westernized Saudis, especially those educated abroad, tend not to use this gesture any longer. The safest bet is simply to copy what a new acquaintance does. Among themselves, Saudi men who know each other well kiss one another on the cheek, but they are perfectly conscious that this is their way and not everyone else's.

A Western man should not offer his hand to a Saudi woman he does not know well, but simply wait to see if she extends her hand. (As above, never try to shake hands

KEY WORDS AND PHRASES

Phrase/word	Meaning in English
Assalamu Alaikum Response: *Wa alaikum assalam*	Peace, be with you (greeting) And also with you (response)
Marhaba	Hello!
Saba-hul-khair Response: *Saba-hul-noor*	Good morning
Masa-hul-khair Response: *Massa-hul-noor*	Good evening
Massalama	Goodbye
Insha'Allah	God willing
Masha'Allah	Praise God / "wow"
Alhamdullilah	Thanks to God
Bokra	Tomorrow (can also mean "early" or "morning")
Walla (also "*Wallahi*")	I swear!
Yalla	Let's go / come on
Khalas	Enough / stop
Ya'ani	I mean . . .
Shukran	Thank you
Mafi mushkila	No problem
Alatool	Right away!

with a woman in the street!) The same applies for foreign women: you shouldn't offer your hand to a Saudi man, but if he offers his hand, it's okay to shake it if you want to. It is becoming more and more common for Saudis to shake hands with opposite gender expats.

The formal greeting is *Assalaamu alaikum*, "Peace be upon you"—to be answered with *Wa alaikum assalaam*, "And peace be upon you." That said, don't be surprised if your carefully practiced Arabic greeting is met with a simple and cheerful "Hi!"

Then there is the more informal hello: *Marhaba* or *Ahlan*—short for *Ahlan wa sahlan*, "Welcome" or more literally "My home and my family (are at your disposal)."

HOSPITALITY AND INVITATIONS

In due course, visitors may find themselves invited to a restaurant or someone's home. Refusal would be considered hurtful unless you have a good excuse and can suggest another time. If you suffer from extreme social phobia, your Saudi acquaintance will probably intuit this and respect your wish to be left alone; otherwise, you should accept the invitation with good grace.

In a restaurant, the host will pay. Saudis who invite you out will take great pride in treating you to dinner, so don't try to "go Dutch" or to pay your portion. Instead, take the opportunity to invite your Saudi host out and return the favor.

On Arrival
Invitations to someone's home offer a chance to experience how important hospitality is to a Saudi. People's behavior can vary widely, so the best thing is to play it by ear rather than arrive with any preconceived notion of a ritual to go through. Visitors should use common sense, and if

they're baffled, ask. Bear in mind that Saudi hosts will make allowances for a guest's cultural background and make adjustments accordingly. There is usually no need to bring a gift, but if you do, it will be graciously received. If you would like to bring something and you're wondering what's appropriate, a sweet treat or dessert is always a good choice. If you have something from your home country, like a box of chocolates, even better; just make sure there's no alcohol or pork gelatine in it.

Most Saudi homes that foreigners are likely to visit will have Western-style furniture (often in a style that has been described as Syrian baroque). A few basic rules: it's customary to take off your shoes when entering the house unless your host is wearing his. If sitting on cushions, don't point the soles of your feet at others. It is generally considered good manners to accept what you are offered.

On arrival, you are likely to be offered a cup of *kahwa*, aromatic coffee from unroasted coffee beans and spices in a thimble of a cup. After one or two cups, the way to indicate that you've had enough is to shake the cup from side to side.

In Saudi houses it was traditional to have a sitting room, called a *majlis*, where men could go to socialize with other men, the entrance of which was around the side or the back of the house. Although many houses still have this room, it is starting to disappear, especially in larger cities where it's now more common for both genders to socialize and eat together. If invited as a couple, you may still find that you are separated on arrival to eat, though chances are slimmer today.

The Meal

Dinner, after a suitable period of sitting around, could be almost anything, but is most likely to be a lavish spread of roast and barbecued meats and the inevitable *kabsa*—spiced rice with meat similar to India's biryani. If you don't know how to eat something, copy your host. There will be too much of everything, so eat heartily but stop when you are full. Your host will press you a little, out of politeness, but there is no force-feeding. Additionally, if you have a food allergy or diet that prevents you from eating something, it's perfectly fine to politely refuse with a short explanation. In the age of globalization and social media, an awareness and acceptance of different dietary preferences is now common in the Kingdom, including diets like gluten-free, ketogenic, and vegan.

In the past, Arabs ate with their hands, using only the right since the left was reserved for personal hygiene. But now many Saudis—and most of those likely to invite foreigners—use cutlery and sit at a dining table. Don't worry too much about infractions of etiquette: your host will probably be far too concerned with your welfare and his duties to even notice.

The meal will probably take some time, culminating in a great variety of sweets. Since Saudis are great storytellers, visitors can leave much of the entertainment to their host, who may regale them with a welter of amusing anecdotes. Again, don't fret: things will be much more relaxed than they would be in a highly socially regimented country like, say, Korea or Japan. Let your host take the lead in the conversation to be on the safe side; most Saudis prefer talking to listening.

There is usually not much after-dinner conversation, so once all the dishes have been cleared away, it is time to think of going home.

TIPS FOR BUILDING RAPPORT WITH SAUDIS

Those from abroad who are working in Saudi Arabia, or for whatever reason are staying in the country for an extended period of time, will find the following tips useful for building rapport with those you would like to befriend.

- There is no substitute for spending time in person. At work, there will likely be invitations to have coffee before or during work, lunch, or dinner together. These are all good chances to show them your personal side and to begin to build bridges.
- For Saudis to feel a connection with you, it's important for them to understand a little about who you are as a person, so don't be afraid to show them some of your true personality—outside of your professional persona.
- Try to find common ground and shared interests. That could be something simple like the same favorite restaurant or sports team, so try to find out about their interests.

In general, Saudis love to talk about football, and since Cristiano Ronaldo has made Saudi his home, it is always a welcome topic of conversation. Beyond that, travel—both within Saudi and abroad—is also a great topic of discussion, especially if you have been to some of the places Saudis dream of visiting. Food and cars are also good and safe topics, as is Vision 2030.

- A display of good public behavior will help endear Saudis toward you. Principally in Saudi Arabia, these are patience, flexibility, and understanding. Humility is also highly esteemed. Yes, it's important to show your professionalism, know-how, and reliability— the trick is to do it without arrogance.

- Appreciation goes a long way, so giving compliments and showing gratitude for someone's help will also contribute to relationship building.

- Saudi is a hierarchical society and the protocols should be followed—going against them will likely only work against you. This extends to general society as much as it does to the workplace. For example, show patience throughout the decision-making process. Expats who are used to being pushy to get things done will need to recalibrate: diplomacy, soft skills, and patience are the tools that are most likely to succeed here.

DATING AND RELATIONSHIPS

If romance blossoms in the desert, be aware that dating in the Kingdom is technically not allowed, as Saudis are expected to marry through family arrangement. However, there is nothing wrong with meeting someone of the opposite sex in a friendly context and in a public place. If a friendship does develop into something more, however, be advised that there are many laws, procedures, and permissions required when marrying Saudis. The rules differ whether the marriage in question is between a Saudi man and a foreign woman, or a Saudi woman and a foreign man, and include salary, age, and health requirements, plus a government application. For example, a Saudi man must be at least forty years old to marry a non-Saudi woman. He must earn at least 3,000 Saudi riyals (SAR) per month and have a suitable home to live in with his new wife. For a Saudi woman marrying a foreign man, she must be at least twenty-five years old, and the age difference between the couple must not be more than thirty years. The foreign man must be able to provide for the financial needs of his Saudi wife and any children they may have and must be able to speak Arabic. He must also be willing to convert to Islam. If you do find yourself in this position, be sure to research all the legal requirements in advance in order to proceed correctly.

CHAPTER FIVE

PRIVATE & FAMILY LIFE

The family is the most important social institution in Saudi Arabia. It is the chief source of identity and the focus of loyalty. Among families, Saudis form a kind of alliance, as between states, based on common interests and lifestyles and usually socialize within this circle.

There are many family businesses, which tend to act as a safety net for all members of the extended family. In companies big and small, many Saudis feel honor-bound to try and find a place for members of their circle.

The oldest male is usually the head of the extended family, and age is respected. Families are often vast, with a small army of children. Large SUVs that can transport the whole family, and with rear windows often blacked out for privacy, are a familiar sight on the Kingdom's roads.

An example of traditional Saudi architecture.

LIVING CONDITIONS

Homes

Jeddah's old town still has some of the traditional, intricately latticed verandas that give this area its old-world charm and feel. Nowadays, with development going on everywhere you turn, much of Saudi Arabia is brand spanking new.

Living conditions in the cities nowadays range from the giant palaces of the royals that stretch over acres of built-up ground, to the sprawling villas and well-appointed mansion flats of the wealthy, to the small, low-income apartments located over shops and fast-food places lining the streets. Marble is readily available and pretty inexpensive.

Compounds and residential apartments in Riyadh's As Sulimaniyah neighborhood.

As we've seen, privacy is a key feature of Saudi life and homes will usually have mirrored or blacked-out windows and walls around the entire house to prevent outsiders looking in. This also plays a role in protecting the honor of a family's womenfolk, who may otherwise be exposed to strangers. Behind the walls of the family home or mini-compound, they are able to go about their business without concern. Inside, homes usually have separate living areas for men and women. How strictly Saudis are segregated varies from family to family.

In most homes, there is a sitting room with an upholstered and cushioned bench running the length of three walls where the host and guests can lounge over tea, coffee, sweets, and a *shisha*. There is often a separate dining area, usually nowadays with a Western-style table and chairs. Most Saudi families will also hire a foreign nanny or housemaid, often from the Philippines, Indonesia, or Africa. The larger the family, the more help is hired.

DAILY LIFE

Daily life revolves around work, family, and religious duties; it is also dictated by the climate. Everything comes to a standstill for the five daily prayers, when shops and restaurants pull their shutters down at the first call. That, rather than the time by the clock, marks the passing of the day. There is a something of a lull in the daily pace

A wide array of fresh produce for sale in Taif.

between the noonday (*dhuhr*) and the sunset (*maghrib*) prayers because for most of the year it is simply too hot to go out. During these hours, most will stay inside, within the comfortable confines of air-conditioned houses and offices.

It's only after *maghrib* that the cities really come to life and families venture out to shop and eat in the relative cool of the evening. Things liven up further after *isha*, the prayer ninety minutes after sunset. Most people eat their family dinner at home after *maghrib* or *isha* and then go for a stroll, or they go to a restaurant at those times.

Expats coming to the Kingdom for the first time will need to get used to these rhythms and plan accordingly. When visiting the shopping malls, some expats bring a book to read while waiting through the evening prayers, which happen twice an evening for around thirty minutes each. To plan ahead for prayer times, you can download an app on your phone which will give you alerts in advance.

Daily Necessities

Food, mostly imported, is in plentiful supply in hypermarkets of American dimensions. Popular supermarket chains include Tamimi, Panda, Carrefour, Danube, and Lulu. From Quaker Oats to sun-dried tomatoes, they stock everything under the sun—except pork—at very reasonable prices. Varieties of fresh meat, vegetables, pickles, cheese, dates, pastries, and other traditional foodstuffs are cheaper and often tastier in the souks. Small neighborhood shops, or *bakalas*, stock a few canned and bagged items. Other necessities are also easily available in any quality and provenance.

Many Saudis now prefer to order their groceries through apps like InstaShop, Nana, Ninja, Jahez, and Carrefour. The popularity of these services grew greatly during the coronavirus pandemic, and new apps are going live all the time, so be sure to check with people in your local area to know which one is the preferred choice.

SOCIAL LIFE

Saudis enjoy social gatherings within their close circle. That can mean just sitting around shooting the breeze over endless cups of tea and *shisha* or, for influential people, a more formal meeting, or *majlis*, where important issues of the day are discussed. Weekends and evenings are usually devoted to the family, be it a picnic, an outing to the families-only amusement parks, or a feast at home.

Informal social gatherings increasingly take place in restaurants or cafés with comfortable lounging areas for groups out of earshot of one another. Such cafés often have giant TV screens that show sports events and music videos. The patrons' *shishas* are topped up from glowing censers until they call for a stop.

Young Saudi women are curious and highly intelligent; many will read whatever they can get their hands on in an effort to further educate themselves, but that doesn't mean that they don't also engage in typical pastimes like shopping and hanging out with their female friends, often

getting together in a café or someone's house to chat the night away.

Fun-loving and adventurous, many young Saudi men engage in drifting, the practice of riding their cars in the desert together and performing stunts. Some even have Friday night "drifting parties," bringing the whole family to the desert to enjoy the events, some of which have turned into competitions like the famous Hail Rally. There was a time when young Saudi men and women couldn't wait for the next chance to take a trip across the border to Dubai or Bahrain. Now, the boredom that once was at home has disappeared, with all the options for entertainment and leisure activities opening up all over the country. For more on the new cultural and entertainment options, see page 136.

CHANGING ATTITUDES

While the family remains the central social unit, younger Saudis are increasingly open to new ways of living and relating to one another that, in general, is seeing the emphasis shift from the collective to the individual. One such example is in the changing attitudes toward marriage. Today more young people are delaying marriage in favor of pursuing higher education and dedicating themselves to career development before choosing to settle down. This is especially the case for women, who now make up the majority of university-level students in the country. As one Saudi friend explained, "Sixty years ago, the age of marriage was between nine and sixteen. Until about twenty years ago, the general age of marriage was in the early twenties. Nowadays, however, it's very common for people to get married in their late twenties and even thirties." So, what is accepted as the norm today would have been highly unusual just decades ago. It is particularly notable when one considers the conservative nature of Saudi society and that these norms were in place for many centuries.

Now, when couples do decide to get married, women often have greater autonomy in family decision-making, and this has contributed to a shift in traditional gender roles outside the home, too. The traditional expectation that several generations will live together is also becoming less common, as more young couples insist on striking out on their own.

Dating

In a society of arranged marriages, dating has always been forbidden, as meeting members of the opposite sex who are not related to you is against cultural norms. However, the advent of the internet has multiplied the avenues for meeting members of the opposite sex. There was a time when young men would write their phone number on a little piece of paper, fold it up and drop it "accidentally" near where a beautiful girl was sitting in a shopping mall. Now, a fleeting encounter in the mall allows them to send their numbers via their phone's Bluetooth. Romance is conducted mainly by text message and through social media. Often it is just an ongoing conversation that goes nowhere.

As previously mentioned, with the easing of social restriction, it is now possible for women and men to socialize together in cafés and to work together. Thus, it is also increasingly likely that one might meet someone special. Dating between Saudis, however, is still nothing like it is in the Western world, with most Saudis still adhering to cultural norms of not having sexual contact before marriage. And if mutual attraction does develop, the man still needs to ask the girl's father for her hand in marriage.

CHAPTER SIX

TIME OUT

How people spend their free time in the Kingdom today is markedly different to how it once was. Once upon a time, foreign expats had to work quite hard to find something to do in the evenings. Thankfully, this is no longer the case and there is now far more available that residents and visitors can take advantage of. For those in the cities, there are cafés, malls, restaurants and *shisha* houses, comedy clubs, movie theaters, concerts, and cultural and sporting events to enjoy. Foreigners working, say, in a university or on one of the Giga Projects, will find multiple options for entertainment in the vicinity that will often include high quality fitness centers, swimming pools, restaurants, beaches, and sometimes movie theaters and bowling alleys. We'll take a closer look at what's now available in this chapter.

Traditional brass coffee and teapots for sale at Souk Al-Zal, Riyadh.

SHOPPING FOR PLEASURE

Souks

The Kingdom's traditional markets, or *souks,* are good for handicrafts from other parts of the greater Middle East—Saudis themselves were traditionally herders, traders, and raiders rather than sedentary craftsmen. What the country does offer is a bewildering variety of dates in all stages from fresh to dried, dipped in chocolate, stuffed with almonds, covered in sesame seeds, and rolled in coconut. All are worth trying.

Bedouin crafts include silver and amber ornaments; the inevitable pewter coffee pots can be picked up here too.

Saudis are lovers of scent, and both men and women use ample musk-based perfume. Homes are scented with traditional *bukhour,* or incense, such as sandalwood (*oud*) chips or oil, heated on coals in distinctive four-sided, "turreted" censers. Whole sections of the downtown *souks* specialize in fragrances: just follow the scent.

DATES

For millennia, these hardy and nutritious fruit were an essential part of the Bedouin diet because they practically never go bad. A handful of dates goes a long way during a desert crossing. In dried form, they have a surprisingly complex taste reminiscent of marzipan.

The oasis of al-Hasa in the Eastern Province is the world's largest date-growing area. Connoisseurs consider the Khalasah, or Khlas, from al-Hasa the best dates in the world. But there is a multitude of regional varieties, which ripen in succession and vary in color from light brown to black. "The first crop is for the emir," the saying goes, "the last for the donkey."

Where other countries donate blankets to the needy, Saudi Arabia donates dates. In 2018, for example, Saudi Arabia donated over seven thousand tons of dates, with four thousand tons going to the World Food Program, and three thousand tons distributed among different countries around the world. It's also common for Saudi workplaces to gift every staff member with a box of dates during the harvest season.

Rugs are also a good buy, from Persian to Afghan. Cheaper varieties are available in dedicated markets, while fine Persian silk carpets from Qom and Isfahan can be found in carpet shops. Expect to spend some time negotiating a reasonable price. In contrast to other parts of the Middle East, there is otherwise not much haggling in the *souk*. Some vendors may offer a small discount of perhaps 5 to 10 percent if asked, but prices are essentially fixed.

Malls

Saudis love their luxury brands, and you find all the upscale shops in Saudi malls like Fendi, Versace, and Prada. For men, there are Boss and Diesel and the like. Top brands often do a special line in *abayas* and *thobes* for their Gulf customers. As luxury brands go, they are quite reasonably priced, and a stroll around the gleaming high-end malls makes a refreshing break from the desert heat.

You can also find mid- to low-range international brands like Zara, Mango, H&M, Victoria's Secret, and GAP, as well as popular international sportwear brands like Nike and Adidas, which are well represented in Saudi malls.

Shoppers at Souq Al-Qaisariah in the eastern city of Al-Hofuf.

TIPPING
....

Tipping culture in Saudi varies depending on who is providing the service. For example, Saudi taxi drivers do not accept cash tips, even when it's a matter of not having the right change and you are happy to let them keep it. They will dig around in every crack between the car seats for the right change to pay you back. Tipping Saudi drivers via your taxi app, however, is acceptable. Taxi drivers of other nationalities accept all tips.

Staff in restaurants and other service-related industries like beauty treatments, massage, etc. are usually expatriates from the Middle East or Asia who depend on tips to make ends meet, so it is a good idea to leave at least 10 to 15 percent.

In offices, it's good practice to tip the tea boys who are most often from Southeast Asia and, like others, send the most part of their salaries back home to support their families. They normally supplement their income by going out to fetch food for you from a nearby shop or making you an extra cup of coffee. Depending on the task, anywhere from 5 to 15 riyals per errand is suitable. There is usually an office collection for them on Eid al-Fitr, too.

In most clothing stores, there are no changing rooms in order to ensure the privacy of women customers. Instead, customers will buy the item, take it home to try on, and return it if it doesn't fit. That said, it's not unheard of for shop assistants to point out a secret changing room in the back for expat shoppers!

For cosmetics, expect to see all your familiar brands like Sephora, MAC, Clinique, The Body Shop, and Bath & Body Works. Electronics, especially from Korea and Japan, are also a good buy, and prices are sometimes a little better than in destinations like Singapore and Bangkok. Home entertainment plays a crucial role in the Kingdom and so all major international brands are present.

MONEY

The SAR, or Saudi Arabian Riyal, remains pegged to the US dollar at a rate of SAR 3.75. All banks exchange dollars to riyals and the other way round, as well as pounds sterling and euros and some other currencies. There are also some exchange centers downtown and in all major airports. SAR can be found in banknotes as well as coins of one and two SAR. The smaller denomination of Saudi money is called "halala," and 100 halala equals 1 SAR. Although still in circulation, halalas are not used much anymore. Indeed, for many, digital payments have become the norm for everything from eating out, groceries, and utility bills. Popular local payment platforms include Moyasar, Payfort, Paytabs, Hyperpay, and STC pay.

EATING OUT

Eating out is widely enjoyed and Saudi's restaurant culture has developed extensively in the last several years. What were meager options in the past have now expanded into a wide variety of restaurant choices that include an array of international cuisines, particularly in the metropolises of Riyadh and Jeddah. In addition to food, many new establishments also offer live music, cultural performances, and other entertainment too.

Particularly popular and reliably delicious is Lebanese cuisine. Readily available, it offers something for every taste and dietary restriction, from meat lovers to vegans to the gluten-intolerant: kebabs, mezze including hummus, *mutabbal* (mashed eggplant), and stuffed vine leaves, *kofta* meatballs, and a range of fresh and zesty salads like *fattoush* and *tabbouli* are some of the highlights.

For a quick lunch on the go, many will pick up a *shawarma*—chicken or lamb cut from the spit and served with spicy sauce and fresh vegetables in a roll of flat bread—which can be found on many a street corner. Vegetarians can opt for falafel, also available in most kebab eateries, or hummus with bread and salad. On the coast, simple restaurants let you choose a fresh fish that is then deep-fried and served with hummus, flat bread, and a salad. Upscale seafood restaurants offer a whole range of delicacies from mussels to lobsters, slow-baked or grilled.

Good, authentic Indian food of regional varieties is plentiful and available from cheap takeaways to upscale and lavish restaurants. Mexican restaurants and Asian food, especially Thai and Japanese, are becoming more popular, and there are plenty of sushi restaurants to choose from. There is also pricey Italian and French food to be had, and Greek food, too.

Then of course there are fast food and "family" restaurants: every franchise under the sun is represented in the Kingdom. Those craving a taste of home can find popular international chains such as Pizza Hut, The Cheesecake Factory, and many more. Cheaper and quicker options like McDonald's and Burger King are widely available.

Traditional Arabian or Bedouin food can be more difficult to find, but there are some "heritage experience" restaurants where you can try camel steak and interesting dishes of roast and stuffed lamb and chicken.

A whole chicken from the spit with rice can be had for SAR 10 in a little Afghan hole in the wall, while a full Lebanese feast in a baroque upscale eatery can cost many hundreds.

When it comes to mealtime, many Saudis are now also opting to have meals delivered to their homes. The most popular food delivery apps are Jahez, Nana, Hunger Station, Careem, and Talabat.

"Saudi Champagne"

Saudi champagne is a nonalcoholic punch of apple juice and sparkling water with plenty of fresh fruit chunks that makes a refreshing drink in the heat and goes surprisingly well with a meal. It's served in most of the better restaurants.

CAFÉ CULTURE

Coffee is a great Arabian tradition, and Saudis have a heroic tolerance for caffeine. Coffee shops are plentiful, and Saudis have their very own variation of Arabic coffee that is yellow in color and spiced with cardamom and saffron. It's yellow because the beans are roasted only briefly, unlike coffee in other parts of the world which is dark brown due to extended roasting of the coffee beans. It is served in tiny cups and is usually poured from an ornate coffee pot. More familiar coffee variations can be had at one of the many international coffee chains that help to keep Saudis sufficiently caffeinated, like Starbucks, Tim Hortons, or Costa Coffee.

Many cafés up- and downtown, indoors and out, concentrate on *shisha*, sometimes with a glass of tea (*chai*) on the side. In groups or alone, Saudis of all classes and

ages love to relax with a *shisha*, topped up constantly by waiters running from table to table with their censers until it's time to go home. Saudi Arabia is a smoker's paradise and *shisha* is the great social lubricant of the whole Middle East. There are many fruit-flavored varieties available among the many tobacco flavors, apple (*tufah*) being perhaps the most popular. Women are just as fond of puffing their *shishas* as men; pretty designs can spark fads, and thousands of riyals are spent on luxury models. Westerners are welcome to take part and local patrons won't bat an eyelid if a visitor sits down among them. The point, after all, is to relax and do what Saudis do best—enjoy the company of others.

THE ENTERTAINMENT REVOLUTION

For much of Saudi Arabia's recent past, entertainment was scarce and limited to family-focused centers and shopping malls. There were few places where the public could gather and mingle. Cinemas were banned in the 1980s, and music concerts were also prohibited. Entertainment options were scarce and often clandestine, with people gathering privately in villas and residential compounds to celebrate an occasion, watch movies, or listen to music. The limited options available included parks, mountain destinations, beach visits, cafes, desert barbecues, farm visits, and shopping malls, which younger generations found lacking. As a result, many Saudis and expats would travel abroad, often to nearby places like Dubai and Bahrain, to enjoy a more relaxed social environment and a wider range of entertainment options. This caused a significant loss of revenue for the Saudi economy.

All this has changed under the Vision 2030, which has eased restrictions to allow for a budding homegrown entertainment industry to take root, and has since received significant funding, all aimed at increasing the quality of life for the country's citizens and residents. To this end, the Saudi government set up the General Entertainment Authority (GEA) to develop and regulate the new entertainment sector.

Movie Theaters

In 2018, Saudi Arabia lifted a thirty-five-year ban on cinema and began opening cinemas throughout the country. The government has since granted licenses to multiple international cinema chains, such as AMC, Vox, and Empire, to open theaters. This was a unique moment in Saudi history that has provided citizens with a new form of entertainment and created jobs in an entirely new sector. The government aims to have over three hundred cinemas with over 2,600 screens in operation by 2030. Growth in Saudi Arabia's film scene is also reflected in the increasing number of cinema festivals and events that are being held. The Red Sea International Film Festival is one such example. It should be noted that films screened in the Kingdom are censored to remove scenes with content that infringe on local cultural norms.

Theater and Performing Arts

Also for the first time in the Kingdom's history, a theater and performing arts scene is developing, supported by

The King Abdulaziz Center for World Culture in Dhahran on the Arabian Gulf.

the Theater and Performing Arts Commission, which provides funding for the creation of new theaters and productions. The Kingdom has also hosted international productions such as Cirque du Soleil and Broadway show tours. The King Abdulaziz Center for World Culture in Dhahran has hosted performances by renowned artists such as Yo-Yo Ma, Lang Lang, and the Vienna Philharmonic Orchestra. The Saudi National Theater Company produces classic plays and in 2020 staged a production of the classic play "Antigone," directed by French director Emmanuel Demarcy-Mota, which featured a cast of both Saudi and international actors.

Interestingly, comedy has also become increasingly popular. There has been a rise in the number of local comedians and the opening of dedicated comedy clubs. The annual Jeddah Comedy Festival is now one of the biggest comedy festivals in the Middle East.

KING SALMAN PARK

King Salman Park is a large park located in the city of Riyadh, which covers an area of over 5 square miles and is one of the largest urban parks in the world.

Attractions of the park include a 1.5-mile-long lazy river, a 40-foot-high waterfall, a roller coaster, a Ferris wheel, and a zipline. There are also playgrounds, sports fields, and picnic areas for families to enjoy.

One of the main highlights of King Salman Park is the cultural village, which showcases the heritage and history of Saudi Arabia through interactive exhibits and traditional performances. Visitors can learn about the country's customs, traditions, and folklore, as well as sample local cuisine and shop for souvenirs.

Music

Music used to be widely frowned upon and the music scene limited to a few famous Saudi singers of opulent ballads that produced songs, as one long-term resident put it, "start with *habibi* (my love) and end with *habibi*." As of 2018, live music concerts were permitted in the Kingdom, and since then it has been host to international pop icons such as Mariah Carey and the Backstreet Boys.

For classical music lovers, the King Abdulaziz Center for World Culture in Dhahran hosts concerts with classical artists and orchestras from abroad. The National

Theater Company produces classic plays, and Maraya in Al Ula has hosted artists of international acclaim like Andrea Bocelli and Alicia Keys.

Just a few years ago, the idea of electronic music and mixed-gender crowds gyrating to pulsing beats in Saudi Arabia would have been unthinkable. But today, one can experience exactly that at the MDLBeast festival. This event attracted more than 600,000 people over four days in 2023, making it one of the largest music festivals in the world. Another music festival is Soundstorm, which has features performances from global electronic music icons such as David Guetta, Tiesto, and Armin Van Buuren.

Musicians performs at the Abqaiq Desert Safari Festival.

QIDDIYA ENTERTAINMENT CITY

Qiddiya Entertainment City is a project currently being constructed in Saudi Arabia that has been billed as the Kingdom's future "capital of entertainment." It will be a vast complex of over 130 square miles (335 sq. km) offering a range of attractions and experiences, including theme parks, water parks, sports facilities, cultural venues, and more. The Qiddiya development is designed to support several Vision 2030 goals, including driving economic diversification, job creation, youth and female empowerment, and doubling household spending on domestic leisure and entertainment.

OTHER CULTURAL ACTIVITIES

Readers can stock up at the Jarir bookstore chain or the Virgin Megastore, which carries a selection of English books. A good variety of English-language books can also be ordered from Amazon Saudi Arabia or Desert Cart, and if you don't find your favorite titles in these shops, you can order from Amazon abroad and have it shipped into the kingdom. Be careful that the topics don't go against Saudi cultural norms: for example, nudity or non-Islamic religious books should not be ordered, as packages may be searched upon arrival and confiscated if they are found to contain offensive material.

Art enthusiasts will be pleased with the extent of works available for viewing in the Kingdom. In the past, the display of artworks was extremely limited owing to the Islamic prohibition on the depiction of living creatures. With the recent easing of restrictions, Saudi has now seen the establishment of numerous galleries including the Athr Gallery, Hafez Gallery, Misk Art Institute, the Saudi Art Council, among others. For the first time in Saudi history, one can also attend art festivals and public exhibitions such as the Riyadh Art Exhibition and Jeddah Art Week.

Foreign embassies and consulates occasionally organize cultural evenings, with lectures on the Kingdom or film screenings. A reliable publication to find out about Arabian culture is *Saudi Aramco World*, the oil giant's in-house magazine whose guest writers are often international experts.

Numerous cultural associations have been set up in recent years that host cultural exchange evenings. One example is Salam for Cultural Communication in Riyadh, where you can attend monthly open events with different themes on culture, which include speakers and networking with food afterwards. For a social club on culture, try the Saudi Culture Club, also in Riyadh.

Picnics

Saudis will picnic anywhere, including the median strip of the coastal highway. On Thursday evenings and on holiday nights, families crowd the sides of certain roads the way Northern Europeans throng to the beaches of the Mediterranean. For a calmer atmosphere and less carbon dioxide, head to one of the landscaped city parks or drive out into the desert for a clear and silent night under the stars.

SPORTS

Vision 2030 includes a commitment to promote healthy and active lifestyles among Saudis, as well as to improve the performance of national athletes in international competitions, and to cultivate the sector to become a more substantial contributor to the national economy. To reach these goals, the Saudi government has invested more than $1.5 billion in developing sports infrastructure and facilities around the country. These include state-of-the-art stadiums, sports academies, and training centers.

Football

Football has always been the centerpiece of Saudi Arabia's sports culture. The national team finally gained recognition when they beat Argentina in the 2022 World Cup, a victory some have called "the biggest surprise in World Cup history." Shortly thereafter, Cristiano Ronaldo's transfer to Saudi Arabia's Al-Nassr Football Club on a two-and-a-half-year contract sent shockwaves through the football world once more. The deal, reportedly worth up to $212 million per year, including commercial agreements, saw the thirty-seven year old become the highest-paid footballer in history and the highest-paid athlete in the world.

Saudi Arabia has set its sights on making the Saudi Premier League one of the top seven leagues in the world. To reach its goal it has invested in the construction of twenty-seven modern football stadiums, and eleven additional modern sports facilities.

Racing

The Saudi Arabian Grand Prix is a recent addition to the Formula 1 calendar. In December 2020, Formula One signed a ten-year deal worth $650 million with Saudi Arabia, which saw the country host its first-ever Grand Prix race in November 2021.

The event takes place in Jeddah on the Jeddah Corniche Circuit, along the city's beautiful waterfront. The circuit is known for its long stretches and sharp corners, and a track layout that demands exceptional skill and precision from drivers. Drivers must also manage their tire wear and energy consumption to ensure optimal performance throughout the race, while navigating a twenty-seven-turn course that leaves little room for error.

Upon launching, the Saudi Grand Prix generated significant international attention and is expected to attract around eighty thousand visitors annually. In addition to the Grand Prix, there are numerous other racing events held throughout the year.

Diriyah ePrix

The Diriyah ePrix is an annual electric car race that takes place at the ancient historical city of Ad Diriyah, a UNESCO World Heritage site. The Formula E race is a double-header event, taking place over two days, typically toward the end of February. The 2,494 km long circuit features twenty one turns, consisting of a mix of tight hairpin curves and fast sweeping bends, making it a challenging track for the drivers. The event draws tens of thousands of spectators annually.

Extreme E Desert Prix
The Saudi Extreme E Desert Prix is an exciting off-road racing event in the rugged beauty of the country's diverse terrain. The inaugural season of the event took place in Al Ula, and for its second season, the Extreme E Desert Prix will move to a new location in NEOM.

The Dakar Rally
The Dakar Rally in Saudi Arabia is a popular off-road racing event that attracts motorsports enthusiasts from

A race car negotiates the challenging terrain of the Dakar Rally.

around the world. The event is organized by the Saudi Arabian Motor Federation and held in vast and challenging desert terrain. The rally has grown in popularity over the years and in 2021, the event saw more than four hundred participants from thirty countries, competing across different categories such as cars, motorcycles, quads, and trucks. Winners take home a $1 million cash prize.

Camel and Horse Racing

Camel and horse racing have a rich history in Saudi Arabia, dating back to the time of the Bedouins. Today they are also a significant contributor to the nation's economy and cultural heritage.

One of the most significant events in Saudi Arabian horse racing is the annual King Abdulaziz Horse Championship, which takes place at the King Abdulaziz Racetrack in Riyadh. With a total prize bank of $20 million, the championship attracts global attention and top competitors from around the world.

The most famous annual camel racing event, the Al Ula Camel Cup, is held in Al Ula and organized by the Royal Commission of Al Ula and the Saudi Camel Racing Federation.

Women in Sports

Before 2018 women were not allowed to enter sports stadiums in Saudi Arabia. Today, not only are women allowed to enjoy public sports events as spectators, but they are also competing. Due to the lifting of restrictions on women's participation in sports and the establishment of women-only sports facilities and events, the Kingdom has seen an increase in the percentage of women engaging

KING ABDULAZIZ FALCONRY FESTIVAL

Falconry has a long and storied history that dates back thousands of years, with evidence suggesting that it was practiced in the Arabian Peninsula as far back as 2000 BC. Over the centuries, falconry has evolved into a symbol of nobility and an essential part of the cultural identity of Saudi Arabia and the wider region.

The annual King Abdulaziz Falconry Festival attracts thousands of falconers, enthusiasts, and spectators from across the globe who come together to witness the incredible skill and finesse of these majestic birds of prey. The event features numerous competitions, demonstrations, and educational workshops. According to figures from the 2021 festival, over four thousand falcons and one thousand seven hundred falconers from eighty countries participated in the event.

Prize falcons are highly sought after in the Kingdom, reflecting the immense value and prestige attached to these birds.

in physical activity; between 2015 and 2021 it rose from 9.5 percent to 23 percent. Saudi women taken part in athletic track events, basketball, football, running, judo, golf, and motorsports.

One woman making headway in this field Princess Reema bint Bandar, Saudi Ambassador to the United States, who is now in the role of Head of the Saudi Federation for Community Sports (SFCS) and the first woman to fulfill this role in Saudi Arabia.

DESERT TRIPS

A trip to the desert is essential to understanding Saudi Arabia. In this majestic silence, the fast pace of city life disappears into silent beauty, and creates the perfect backdrop for stargazing, family barbecues, bonfires, and long walks. And thanks to the desert, lovers of off-road driving have a playground twice the size of Western Europe on their doorstep. The Empty Quarter, or Rub al-Khali, covers an area greater than France of—as the name suggests—nothing but rock, sand, and salt flats. Spectacular sand dunes can rise over 984 feet (300 m). In the far east are quicksands that have allegedly swallowed entire caravans.

For more ambitious desert trips, it is vital to travel in groups. People still die out here when they get lost or run out of gas, even though highways now skirt or cross the wastes. Travel with at least two 4WD vehicles and never without a local guide. Drive off-road only if you are sure of your driving skills, and never too far. Carry more water and gas than you think necessary and bring a shovel. The best option is to book through a travel agency that specializes in such trips. Or drive on safe highways not too far out of the cities for a glimpse: even several miles out of town and a few hundred yards from the road, the experience can be breathtaking. Bear in mind that the nights can get very cold, so bring warm clothes and a sleeping bag.

DIVING

The Red Sea on the western coast has some of the best diving in the world, with unspoiled coral reefs stretching for miles up and down the coast. Diving here is very popular among expatriates, and there are plenty of diving clubs. These are mostly found on private beaches that are also a convenient place to meet people—and where bathing in swimming trunks or a bikini is not a problem. The Red Sea is also one of the best places in the world to learn to scuba dive; comparatively it's very affordable, the instructors highly trained, and the underwater terrain beautiful. Many divers also point out that it's a very safe diving environment, with low numbers of sea creatures that can harm you compared to other places. Warm weather year-round means you can go diving whenever you want.

CHAPTER SEVEN

TRAVEL, HEALTH, & SAFETY

The Kingdom of Saudi Arabia is a treasure trove of ancient ruins, cultural landmarks, and more than thirty thousand archaeological sites where the land's rich past can be explored. For much of the country's history, these sites were all but closed off to the outside world. Travel to the Kingdom was for the most part restricted to business or religious purposes. That all changed in 2019, when an eagerly awaited Tourist Visa was introduced as part of the country's Vision 2030. Within the first day, no less than seventy-seven thousand people signed up for the new visa.

At the time of writing, Saudi's online eVisa application system allows visitors from forty-nine countries to apply for a multiple-entry visa online that is valid for ninety days over the course of a year.

The eVisa application process is straightforward: submit an application with relevant visit details at visa.visitsaudi.com, pay the fees, and get approved online.

It's important to note that this visa doesn't allow visitors to take part in Hajj, study, or work-related activities. Alternative visa options include a Business Visit Visa, Employment Visa, and Temporary Work Visa. More information about each visa type can be found at vc.tasheer.com, where applications can also be made.

LGBTQ TRAVELERS

A 2023 article published by CNN entitled "Saudi Arabia Welcomes LGBTQ Visitors" caught the international community quite by suprise. And indeed, according to the FAQ section of the Saudi Tourism Authority's official website, Visit Saudi, "Everyone is welcome to visit Saudi Arabia and visitors are not asked to disclose such personal details."

This of course must be understood within the context of Saudi Arabia's cultural norms. Saudi is an extremely private society and a person's romantic life is part of the personal realm and kept out of public life. The same discretion is expected of all couples. Heterosexual or otherwise, no public displays of affection are allowed, except for holding hands. Basically, one's personal life should remain private and kept out of public view. With this in mind, no visitor that follows this rule will encounter problems in Saudi Arabia.

Architectural sights abound in Al-Balad, the historic center of Jeddah city.

PLACES TO VISIT

Hejaz Region

The Hejaz region, situated on the western side of Saudi Arabia, is home to cities Mecca, Medina, Jeddah, Tabuk, Yanbu, Taif, and Baljurashi. This region is referred to as the Western Province and shares borders with the Red Sea to the west, Jordan to the north, Najd to the east, and the Region of 'Asir to the south. The Hejaz is the most diverse region in the Arabian Peninsula, and its largest city, Jeddah, is also the second largest city in Saudi Arabia. Mecca and Medina also hold positions as the fourth and fifth largest cities in the country, respectively.

Jeddah City

Jeddah is a vibrant and exciting city. Located on the Red Sea coast, it is known for its stunning beaches, bustling markets, and exotic restaurants. It is also home to a thriving business district and a variety of tourist attractions.

The old city of Jeddah (Al-Balad) is a must-see
for visitors to the city. This historical district dates
back centuries and is full of interesting architecture,
traditional mosques, and colorful souks. There are many
museums in Al-Balad that showcase Arabian culture
and history, including the famous King Fahd Fountain.
Visitors can also explore the historic Hejaz Railway
Station or relax in one of Al-Balad's many parks and
gardens. Jeddah has something to offer everyone,
from shopping, sightseeing, and dining to adventure
activities like scuba diving and safari tours.

Mecca (Makkah) Province

Mecca was the birthplace of Prophet Mohammed. The
holiest city for Muslims, it hosts millions of pilgrims
each year who visit to perform the Hajj pilgrimage,
one of the five pillars of Islam. The history of Mecca
dates back over one thousand four hundred years when
the Prophet Mohammed founded Islam. The city is
mentioned in the Qur'an as the birthplace of Islam,
and the sacred Kaaba, a cube-shaped building located
within the Grand Mosque, is Islam's holiest site. Mecca
is believed to be the site where Adam and Eve met after
being expelled from the Garden of Eden, and where
Prophet Mohammed began receiving revelations from
the Angel Gabriel and preaching the teachings of Islam.
The city is also considered the spiritual center of the
Islamic world.

It should be noted that only Muslims are permitted
to enter the city of Mecca. It is considered a matter of
religious sensitivity and non-Muslims are not allowed to

Mecca, the birthplace of the Prophet Mohammed.

enter under any circumstances. The authorities do
take efforts to identify and turn away non-Muslims.

King Abdullah Economic City (KAEC)

KAEC is a megaproject located one hundred kilometers
north of Jeddah. Here tourists can relax on the beautiful
Yam Beach, take a boat cruise along the Red Sea shore,
explore the natural beauty of Juman Park, or spend
an evening at the Seaside Clubhouse. KAEC also has
numerous restaurants where visitors can sample
delicious local cuisine.

Taif City

Taif is a unique city known for its rose gardens,
mountains, and monkeys that roam freely throughout the
city. A day trip to Taif can include a ride on a cable car
with stunning mountain views, visits to heritage villages
showcasing Saudi village culture of the past, and a front-
row seat at camel races. Being at higher altitude, Taif is

Traditional weaving at Taif's historic Souk Okaz.

also loved for its cooler climate. The best time to visit is in March and April, when the roses are in full bloom. Delicious pomegranates, apricots, and rose-flavored products can be bought at local markets here. If you decide to feed the monkeys, beware—they can be quite vicious!

Tabuk Province

Tabuk province is located in the northwest of the country and is bordered by Jordan in the north, and the Red Sea to the west. The area is full of natural beauty and history, and the Red Sea is a popular destination with crystal-clear waters, vibrant sea life, and some of the world's best coral reefs.

NEOM, the Kingdom's largest and most famous Vision 2030 Giga Project, is a must-see. The site offers a unique climate with beaches and snow-capped mountains. The futuristic city has a variety of attractions, including unique architectural projects and cultural sites. For more on the NEOM Giga Project, see page 37.

For those who love hiking and adventure, Bajdah is a worthwhile destination with breathtaking views of lush green hills. Wadi Dissah features dramatic rock formations and a tranquil lake, the perfect destination for a picnic or peaceful retreat. Wadi Tayib Ism is home to fertile valleys nestled between towering mountains, ideal for those seeking a glimpse of authentic Saudi Arabian village life. For those who love beaches, Umluj is known as one of the best beach locations in the country. For the history buffs, Tayma boasts fascinating ruins and ancient settlements.

Medina Province

Medina Province is situated between the Red Sea and the Najd. This province contains the holy city of Medina, which is one of the most important places for Muslims around the world. Apart from its religious significance, it also has a rich cultural history that dates back centuries. It was considered to be an important stop on ancient caravan routes.

Besides Medina City, visitors to Medina Province can explore the historic sites of Khaybar and Al-Ula, an ancient oasis and a UNESCO World Heritage Site with ancient rock carvings created by the Nabataeans, the same civilization that created Petra in Jordan. Besides visiting the ancient ruins, tourists can go hiking, camping, bird watching, and enjoy adventure activities. Concerts, exhibitions, conferences, and other events take place in the iconic mirrored grand venue Maraya.

Beach-lovers should make a point of visiting Yanbu, a port city located along the Red Sea coast, where pristine beaches, coral reefs, and colorful marine life can be found in abundance.

Southern Region

The Southern Region includes many areas worth exploring, among them Asir, Al Baha, Jazan, and Najran.

Asir province has two main cities of interest to travelers, Abha and Rijal Almaa. Abha is the capital of Asir Province and is located 1,200 meters above sea level. The city offers a surreal panorama with views of the Harrat Al Birk volcano field. Rijal Almaa is home to hundreds of rare plant species that beautify its ecosystem with cool temperatures in spring to mid-summer.

Al-Baha is a city covered in clouds. It tends to be quite humid but makes up for it with stunning forests and green mountain summits. At an altitude of 800 meters, Al-Baha also has modern luxury inns for tourists, as well as fine dining restaurants where visitors can enjoy local desert dishes.

The historic village of Rijal Almaa in Asir Province.

Najran is located on the Yemen border and has a history of settlement going back four thousand years. The city was occupied by the Romans and is known as the first place Christians lived in southern Arabia. Places worth visiting are the Najran Valley Dam, the Castle of Rome, Aan Palace, and Emara Palace.

North Central Region

This region includes the provinces of Jawf, Ha'il, and Qassim. The region's largest city, Ha'il, is home to many interesting sights and attractions, including the Seven Sisters—seven large sandstone formations that are over one thousand years old. These unique formations are considered to be one of the most beautiful natural sites in the country. Additionally, visitors can explore Mount Shammer to the north and Mount Salma to the south, both of which offer stunning views of the surrounding landscape. Finally, there are numerous rock art sites in Ha'il province that date back thousands of years and provide insight into the ancient cultures of the region.

Central Region

Saudi's Central Region is home to the vibrant capital city Riyadh, known for its stunning architecture, bustling financial district, and diverse culinary scene. Highlights of the city include Riyadh Boulevard, a popular shopping destination that features more than one hundred and sixty retail stores and restaurants, as well as the Kingdom Tower, a towering skyscraper that is the centerpiece of the financial district. The city is also home to the Riyadh Safari, a sprawling wildlife reserve

Riyadh city, the capital of Saudi Arabia.

that is home to a wide variety of animals from around the world including lions, tigers, and giraffes.

One of the Kingdom's most breathtaking natural sights is located just outside of Riyadh: The Edge of the World. This stunning geological formation offers a panoramic view of the surrounding desert landscape and is a popular destination for hikers and adventurers. Another popular outdoor destination in Riyadh is the Musayqirah hiking trail, which offers visitors the chance to experience the beauty of the region's rock formations and desert landscape up close. Finally, visitors to the area should be sure to explore the historic Darb Al-Manjur, a historic mountain path that dates back to the Ottoman period.

Eastern Region

The Eastern Region, also known as the Eastern Province, is something of a hidden gem. The largest region of the country, it is full of cultural sites and stunning scenery to explore. One of the top attractions is the Ithra in

Dhahran, a cultural hub that hosts festivals, workshops, exhibits, and performances from local and international artists. There are numerous galleries showcasing modern and contemporary art, a library with over two hundred thousand books, and a cinema. Visitors to the library can learn more about the history of Eastern Province, and resources can be found in multiple languages, including Arabic, English, and French.

Another must-visit site is Fanateer Beach in Jubail, famous for its crystal-clear waters, soft white sand, and scenic sunset views. There are also plenty of activities for visitors to enjoy, including diving and paddleboarding. In spring, visitors can witness the world-famous migration of the Hawksbill sea turtles.

Visitors to the region should also check out the charming Al Hofuf city, famous for its historic caves, waterfalls, and fascinating rock formations.

GETTING AROUND

Roads and Traffic

Saudi Arabia is a country of cars, and roads are one of the Kingdom's great prides. Main roads in the cities often have eight lanes or more, and well-maintained highways connect all the major points of the vast territory.

There was a time, not so long ago, when oil was cheaper than water, and although gasoline is still inexpensive, the price has surpassed that of water.

Traffic in the cities tends to clog at peak times, and although the jams are not quite as bad as other megacities in Asia, Riyadh is well on its way to reaching that level, especially around rush hour. Be aware of reckless drivers and road accidents, as road death statistics are pretty high despite the relatively low population density. During the high season of Hajj, traffics jams in and around Mecca and Medina are common, and public transportation is often overcrowded. The road quality outside main cities varies so be aware of potholes or sudden sandstorms that can cover the streets with a blanket of sand.

Taxis

Nowadays, internationally popular hail-a-ride apps operate in Saudi's main cities, Uber, Careem, and Bolt being the most popular. It's a good idea to have these apps on your phone because it's not always possible to hail a taxi on the street, even in busy Riyadh. Though it is the most expensive, Uber perhaps offers the safest service as it only uses Saudi drivers who are verified. Other apps feature both Saudi and non-Saudi drivers who may or may not have gone through a verification process.

PUBLIC TRANSPORTATION

Buses

Most Saudi cities now offer numerous public bus routes. Saudi Public Transport Company (SAPTCO) operates Riyadh Bus, a comprehensive network that covers most parts of the city as well as a fleet of more than four thousand five hundred buses along routes throughout the country.

The Haramain High Speed Railway transports passengers in the provinces of Mecca and Medina.

Metros

The Riyadh Metro, currently in the final stages of construction, will service eighty-five station across six lines. Running a total length of more than 100 miles (160 km) it will be one of the largest metro systems in the Middle East. A metro system in Jeddah is also under construction and is expected to be completed in the coming years. The Jeddah Metro will have four lines and service eighty-six stations.

Trains

A number of Saudi Arabia's cities are connected via rail lines. Medina, Jeddah, and Mecca are connected by the Haramain High Speed Rail and has a journey time of two hours and thirty minutes. Riyadh and Jeddah are connected by the North-South Railway and is a six-hour journey.

In one of Vision 2030's many futuristic plans, Virgin Hyperloop is building a series of high-speed tunnels across Saudi Arabia. The super-fast low-pressure tunnels will transport passengers at speeds of over 1000 kilometers an hour; the journey from Jeddah to Mecca will be completed in just five minutes, and from Riyadh to Jeddah in just forty-six minutes (it currently takes just under two hours by plane).

Air

Currently, the easiest way to get around the Kingdom is by air. Saudi Arabian Airlines (Saudia), Flynas, and Flyadeal operate plenty of affordable daily flights between all major and some minor cities. For trips to more out-of-the-way destinations, the best option is to fly to the nearest airport and rent a car.

For travel to other countries in the Gulf, Middle East, and further afield there are numerous international routes serviced daily by Saudia, Emirates, Air Arabia, and Flynas.

ACCOMMODATION

Short Term

Many major five-star international chains have hotels in the metropolitan areas of Riyadh, Jeddah, and Al-Khobar–Dammam. International websites and apps like Booking.com, Hotels.com, and Expedia.com are popular locally. Airbnb is also active and flourishing in Saudi Arabia. Good independent hotels in more out-of-the-way destinations like al-Jouf are worth the time taken to research online or can be booked via travel agencies.

Long Term

Accommodation for Western expatriates is usually in compounds, though villas and apartments are also easy to rent for those who fancy being closer to the everyday life of the cities. Compounds run the gamut from very basic to swank and are popularly built in a sort of Canary-Island Andalusian style, like a retirement complex. They usually have plenty of facilities such as pools and gyms as well as staff to assist residents with everything from landscaping to maintenance.

Rent in a compound is several times more expensive than outside. In most cases, this won't matter for Western expatriates whose housing costs are most often covered by their employer but can be a consideration for those paid a housing allowance. Life in the cities is perfectly safe, and an apartment can be a good option for people who like to keep to themselves.

Availability in compounds can be explored at rightcompound.com. Those who prefer to look for an apartment can use ksa.aqarmap.com/en or the associated Aqarmap app.

HEALTH

At the risk of stating the obvious, it must be made clear that Saudi Arabia is a very hot country. The coast is hot and humid, while inland is hot and dry, so it's essential to drink plenty of bottled water to avoid dehydration and to not sit around in the midday sun, when severe sunburn can occur in a matter of minutes for those of fair complexion. Food is usually safe to eat, though the odd bout of diarrhea is not unknown. Stock up on charcoal tablets and rehydration salts. Sandstorms can dry out the mucous membranes and cause respiratory complaints.

If you wear contact lenses, you may also want to make sure you carry a pair of glasses with you. The sand and hot temperatures dry out eyes pretty quickly. Plus, if sand blows into your eyes while wearing contacts, it can be very painful or at the least, cause irritation. Some expats have found switching to wearing glasses full time more comfortable while working in Saudi Arabia.

To obtain a work permit, expatriates are legally required to produce a number of medical tests. The list of tests required differs according to country of origin, and may include HIV, Hepatitis B and C, tuberculosis, a pregnancy test, a chest x-ray, and other exams. The World Health Organization (WHO) recommends vaccinations for diphtheria, measles, mumps, rubella, polio, and hepatitis B, though they are not required.

Health care in the many gleaming new hospitals is generally good. Doctors are either expatriates themselves or Saudis trained abroad. Nurses tend to be Filipinos and Filipinas who are highly trained and very efficient. If you are here to work, your health insurance cover will come with a list of approved hospitals. Ask colleagues which one they favor. Pharmacies are plentiful and well-stocked. Many medicines can be obtained without a prescription, by just explaining your problem to the pharmacist.

Outside the major cities, health care can sometimes be hard to find, so on excursions it is a good idea to keep a basic medical kit in the car.

SAFETY

Saudi Arabia has long had one of the lowest crime rates in the world: the Gallup Law and Order Index ranked Saudi in the world's top ten safest countries. It was also placed in the top three safest countries by the UN's Institute of Environment and Human Security. Women who relocate to the Kingdom alone will encounter no problems traveling around by themselves.

Violent crime is extremely rare, as are property crimes such as theft and burglary. In fact, you will find that people often leave their belongings alone in public places knowing that no one will touch them. There are strict laws against drug-related crimes. Possession and trafficking both incur extremely harsh penalties for offenders.

The crimes to be more wary of nowadays, as in many places around the world, are cybercrimes such as hacking, identity theft, and fraud. Also be careful of pickpocketing and purse snatching in crowded areas such as fairs and festivals, including during Hajj and Umrah. Finally, exercise caution and check travel advisories if traveling within 50 miles of the Saudi-Yemen border, which includes the cities of Abha, Jizan, Najran, and Khamis Mushayt.

CHAPTER EIGHT

BUSINESS BRIEFING

If in the past doing business in Saudi Arabia was a trying endeavor, today that is no longer the case. There are now a number of considerable incentives to work, live, and do business in the Kingdom. Vision 2030 has created a plethora of investment opportunities, new business ventures, and openings for partnership with the government, the Giga Projects, and the private sector. It has also become much easier to register a new business, and numerous companies and government agencies are now available to assist in the process.

For those coming to work in the Kingdom, there are differences to be aware of, such as in communication style, in ways of thinking and problem solving, as well as in attitudes toward risk, hierarchy, and conflict resolution—to name just a few. There are also the rhythms of Saudi society that one must become attuned to, such as different high and low periods, and different consumer behavior. As one coffee shop owner noted, "In the UK, peak time for coffeeshops may be 10 a.m., but in Saudi, it's 9 p.m.!"

SAUDI TIME

There was a time in the not-so-distant past when those doing business in Saudi Arabia were often frustrated by the time it took to get things done. Today, it's more accurate to say that a variety of attitudes toward timeliness exists, often depending on the type of organization in question. For example, the speed that things will move at in an institution like a university or a government organization will differ greatly to that of a private company. Despite people's best intentions, long delays can still be a common feature among larger organizations, and this is most often due to hierarchies that continue to play an important role in Saudi business culture. Often the person you're likely to deal with on a day-to-day basis is not the one who has the power to make decisions. They must wait for the go-ahead from superiors, which causes inevitable delays.

It can be difficult for expats to comprehend the often-unseen dynamics that govern decision-making and that may sometimes cause progress to grind to a halt. If something has become urgent, your best bet is to follow up, multiple times if necessary. When doing so, always maintain complete politeness. As you will be aware by now, honor is extremely important in Saudi society, so always be courteous so as not to embarrass anyone, particularly not in front of others. Some expats have found that insisting too much can also backfire and result in complete inaction. Saudis don't appreciate drama in the office and so it's always wise to use diplomacy and soft skills, no matter how urgent the request.

HIERARCHY

Saudi businesses tend to be very hierarchical. As we've seen, this means that decisions often take time as every question and approval has to go through the entire chain of command—and come back down. You may find that decisions become stuck for long periods, and all that's missing is a signature from the Big Boss. It's also common for things to progress suddenly after a long wait.

In Saudi businesses, there is a considerable gap between workers and decision-makers. Geert Hofstede, the renowned intercultural theorist, called this dynamic "power distance." Saudi Arabia is a culture that typically has a large power distance in organizations, meaning a greater separation between staff and those in decision-making positions. Then there is often a carefully constructed system of approvals and chain of command. It should be noted that despite this dynamic, decisions can move quickly by approaching the right person with an urgent but respectful inquiry.

WASTA

Wasta is an Arabic word meaning "connections" or "influence." It's a dynamic that exists in every society to varying degrees—some would say it's human nature. In Saudi society, having connections and relationships with the right people was paramount. If your application was stuck, perhaps due to the heavy bureaucracy that once characterized business in the Kingdom, you could call a friend at the relevant office and your application was likely to be processed the same day.

In the past, it was common to talk openly about *wasta*, and to ask someone to "lend you" their *wasta* in a time of need. Nowadays, though personal relationships are still important, one should approach the topic of *wasta* with discretion. As Saudi has modernized, there has been a marked reduction in nepotism, cronyism, and corruption, and the *wasta* system that sometimes contributed to it has become less acceptable.

One example of how *wasta* is fading out is in the hiring processes for jobs. More and more, Saudis in high positions decline to hire people who came through a *wasta* channel. Many employers no longer subscribe to the mindset of hiring only those you know, or those who came through someone you know.

It may still be possible to make use of a recommendation, but you can now expect that there will be full scrutiny of your candidature and that you will be judged on your merits rather than who you know.

As one Saudi professional pointed out to me, Vision 2030 has gone a long way to replacing the old *wasta* system with one that is more meritocratic, and that young Saudis in particular, having seen its benefits, are in favour of this shift.

GREETINGS AND RESPECT

Saudis show great respect for their superiors. One outward expression of this is that employees will stand

up in the presence of the boss and it's good practice
for expats to do the same, though Saudis are generally
forgiving of newcomers. They understand that Westerners
are not necessarily aware of all the local customs
and are extremely tolerant of our relative ignorance.
Interestingly, some Saudis appreciate the lack of ceremony
in the Western business world and may welcome the
opportunity for an informal chat.

It is polite to address Saudis by their title. If they have
a Ph.D., be sure to call them "Doctor"; otherwise they
are Mr., followed by the first name, for example, Mr.
Mohammed or Dr. Said.

You will notice that there are also other titles given to
people that don't exist in the Western world, for example,
"Eng." means "Engineer" and similar to "Mr." and "Dr."
should proceed the first name when speaking to him
or introducing him (for example, "Engineer Khalid").
Also, the title H.E. before someone's name stands for
"His Excellency" or "Her Excellency" and is used for
someone who is a high-ranking government official or
ambassador. Once again, the title should be spoken before
the first name of the person. The title "H.H" means "His
Highness" or "Her Highness" and comes before the name
of a member of the royal family. When addressing them
directly, you would use "Your Excellency" and "Your
Highness," respectively. One exception is the King
of Saudi Arabia who is given a special religious title
"The Custodian of the Two Holy Mosques."

Hands are shaken at meeting and parting, but not
across genders. At the beginning of business dealings
people will be extremely formal, but as they become

more familiar with one another, they may greet their colleagues and superiors by calling them "Abu Ahmed," meaning "father of Ahmed," in the case of a male colleague whose son's name is Ahmed. Women who come to work in Saudi can expect the same respectful treatment that their male counterparts receive.

Remember that etiquette works both ways: while visitors should make all reasonable efforts not to offend their hosts, they need not put up with too much nonsense either. In certain contexts, especially with an employer or landlord, being firm can help establish the respect that you deserve. Losing your temper, however, is not a good idea.

BUSINESS ETIQUETTE

Tea and Coffee

When doing business in the Middle East one can't underestimate the importance of small cups of rich, yellow coffee. Indeed, it would be rude to get straight down to brass tacks. Saudis enjoy lengthy conversation, so visitors and expatriates can expect to spend a considerable time chatting before what feels like "getting on with business," but for Saudis the preamble is an integral part of the process, so try not to rush things.

It is common for people to answer phone calls, deal with other visitors, and address other duties during your visit; this is all perfectly normal. Let your Saudi boss or business partner set the pace, unless it goes on for too long.

Even when there is a big meeting or negotiation with foreign visitors, it may be flanked by smaller, informal chats over tea in the boss's office. Here, the democratic nature of Saudi society asserts itself—a trace of tribal custom and the obligation of Islamic rulers to be available to hear their people's complaints.

Another great catalyst for establishing friendly relations in business is what Graham Greene called the "ordeal by tea": glass after glass of black tea sweetened with at least two lumps of sugar, sometimes flavored with a leaf or two of mint, is drunk in offices almost nonstop, perhaps varied after evening prayer with a cup of strong Turkish coffee.

Business Dress

Saudi men are properly dressed when they wear a *thobe* and sandals, though in many offices they wear closed shoes and socks; even those who otherwise dress in jeans and shirt for work will wear a *thobe* for important meetings. Men of higher status often dress in particularly fresh, pressed *thobes*, and a white *ghutra* or *keffiyeh* instead of the checkered red-and-white *shummagh*.

Western men should wear suits and ties, or at least a long-sleeved, button-down shirt, tie, dress pants, and dress shoes. Expat women can wear business attire with an *abaya* over it. The *abaya* can be open, and even though wearing it is no longer legally required, doing so out of respect makes a good impression, particularly in formal contexts.

Women who choose not to wear an *abaya* should make sure their clothes are in line with local norms. Sleeves should reach the elbow at least, and shoulders should be covered (so no sleeveless shirts and no wide-neck shirts that may accidentally droop on one side and expose a bare shoulder). Typical business attire like collared, button-down shirts, suit jackets, and dress pants are common, but none should be too tight. Likewise, be sure that clothes are not transparent and that shirts are not low-cut. Skirts should be long, and fall below the knee, and of course no crop tops, exposed midriff, bra strap, or pants that are too tight.

Everyone, male or female, must wear formal clothes when entering any government office in Saudi Arabia. That means a *thobe* for Saudi men, a suit and tie for expat men, and a closed *abaya* for women.

A Matter of Respect

A European engineering project company was collaborating with a Saudi client on a large, long-term, and multimillion dollar project. Some members of the Saudi team came to spend a few months in Europe to oversee the project. They began having weekly meetings which started with a briefing delivered by a woman from the European side. This woman came to the first meeting wearing a low-cut shirt and tight, short skirt. The Saudi Project Manager spoke to the Project Manager, asking him to kindly request the woman to dress appropriately for meetings. The next meeting, the woman defied the request and arrived dressed in the same way as before. The Saudi team stood up and walked out of the meeting, and subsequently removed the woman from the project.

Socializing

The Saudis take great pride in their hospitality. This includes in business, where they will put on a generous spread for important business visitors, usually in a five-star hotel. New employees are also often taken out for a meal by their boss. There are special occasions—something like office Christmas parties back home but rather more sober—where companies invite their staff and families to a hotel, upscale restaurant, or catered event. A favorite is the lavish *iftar* feast at sundown during Ramadan.

Such events are informal, enjoyable, and well worth attending, but there is none of the compulsion of a country like Japan, where failure to show is practically a sackable offense. Dressing neatly in a shirt and tie is appreciated.

MEETINGS

Saudis have warmed to the practice of exchanging business cards and will have theirs handy; so should visitors, as it helps establish credibility. Many business cards are printed in Arabic on one side and English on the other. Expatriates may be provided with such a card by their company. Be sure to check the information before giving the go-ahead for a print run of thousands.

Meetings—and certainly in-company meetings—may proceed with or without a written agenda, depending on the organization. The custom is for the senior Saudi, who will be seated at the head of the table, to speak at some length and then open the discussion to others. Take your cue from him.

Formal meetings start more or less on time and tend to get straight down to business. Punctuality is appreciated, but there is some flexibility.

Saudis listen better in one-to-one meetings, but the irony is that one-to-one meetings are not very common. According to Saudi labor law, for the protection of women, meetings between workers of opposite genders must be conducted with the door kept open or in a place with clear glass walls. Otherwise, there should be three people present.

PRESENTATIONS

Presentations are common and will be expected, usually with a well-prepared PowerPoint file. Meeting rooms in most Saudi workplaces are fully equipped and it should be easy to arrive with your laptop, plug in, and start presenting.

It's important to have a clean, professional appearance with proper business dress, and to state your qualifications at some point in the presentation to establish credibility. Your reputation (or your company's) will play an important role in convincing people. Be sure to show respect and use the proper titles as previously mentioned.

Saudis are attentive listeners but will interrupt when excited. It's normal for them to become quite theatrical, and this sometimes includes raising their voices. This isn't anger, but enthusiasm.

Where possible, try to keep presentations short, because Saudis can get impatient if too many details are included, and presentations become drawn out. As such, it's best to summarize any written slides and material with bullet points. An interactive presentation style works best, since Saudi culture is highly verbal. They will listen intently and welcome the chance to discuss things and ask questions, and the interaction will mean more engagement on their part.

A Personal Touch

An American businessman who was presenting to a group of potential partners in Saudi Arabia was advised to add a personal touch to his presentation. Knowing Saudi is a very family-oriented society, he decided to include a photo of his family. The only problem was that the photo of a family vacation showed his teenage daughter wearing a crop top revealing her midriff. When adding personal information, take care that it does not offend Saudi cultural norms.

NEGOTIATIONS

It's rare for negotiations to be conducted in a single concentrated session. They are usually a lengthy process around a centerpiece formal meeting, or meetings, of the two sides. That process also includes informal chats over tea or coffee in the office and perhaps the intercession of third parties who will have a word in this or that ear.

Plan ample time to spend on this process, or better still prepare to make several trips.

That is not to say that the big meeting, when it comes, will not have to be thoroughly prepared. Be sure to study the company and the stakeholders in detail prior to the event. It's best to show up to the meeting with your side's decision-maker, and ask them to bring theirs. An even temper and a sense of humor are absolutely essential, and a show of overconfidence or arrogance would alienate your hosts. Saudis prefer to feel comfortable with a business partner.

Saudis are skilled negotiators by nature, so be sure to plan a strategy with your team but be ready to give concessions. It's important to have a margin for offering discounts. Many companies who have done business in Saudi Arabia took a hit in the beginning but found it to be very worthwhile in the long run. Most Saudis are interested in win-win and long-term growth, so patience is needed for investing in the relationship and cultivating your partnerships.

It's important to show solidarity among your team. Be careful not to argue in front of the other party; it may be seen as a weakness. Make sure to write down all the meeting's details and send a follow-up email shortly thereafter. If there is no response to your email, be ready to pick up the phone or schedule another meeting.

CONTRACTS AND FULFILLMENT

You may find that contracts written by Saudis will be brief, high-level summaries, and contain much less detail than contracts from other countries. Even if the Saudi side asks your company to write and provide the contract, it will be expected to be brief.

In Saudi business collaborations, it's the relationship that counts more than the piece of paper. Honor requires that someone sticks to their word. Continued contact is also important; a long silence can be more deadly for a business relationship than a heated argument, so keep in touch and maintain an exchange of friendly tokens.

The same goes for the employment contracts of Western expatriates. They can of course expect to be paid on time, in full, and should tolerate no delays. But any other issues are open to renegotiation without a new document needing to be drawn up. Never fear: Saudi employers are extremely unlikely to dishonor the new agreement. In fact, due to the patron–client relationships Saudis maintain, Western expats often find that the reality of their employment is more favorable than the paper contract stipulates.

SETTLING DISPUTES

In disputes, it is a good idea to blame third parties or fate rather than a Saudi partner, even if it is clear to both sides who is really at fault. If the fault is yours, however, Saudis will value a sincere apology.

Even in serious disputes, it's worth trying to work things out informally rather than resorting to lawyers. Don't be afraid to try different techniques, for example, speaking to someone who is likely to pass on the message. You may also try bringing your emotions into the situation. Unlike other countries where there is an implicit rule to remove one's emotions from the sphere of work, use of emotions can appeal to Saudis as they themselves are highly emotional. Whatever you do, make sure not to insult a Saudi partner face to face.

Once a disagreement is settled, you can usually count on your relationship going back to the state it was in before the argument, and Saudis will often act as if nothing has happened. The law—that is, the commercial or labor courts—should be the last resort.

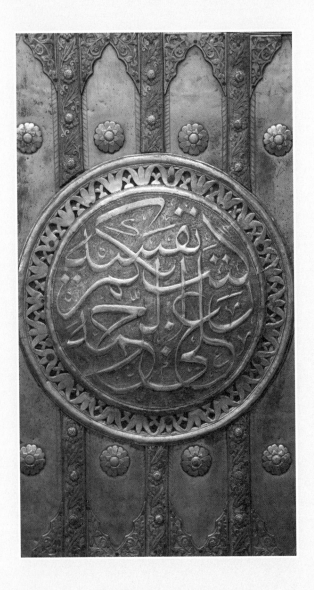

CHAPTER NINE

COMMUNICATING

LANGUAGE

Arabic is a Semitic language belonging to the Afro-Asiatic language family. As a language spoken by over 420 million people worldwide, it has significant cultural and historical importance. Classical Arabic is the language of the Qur'an and remains the foundation of MSA (Modern Standard Arabic), the standardized form of Arabic. You will find MSA used in formal contexts such as news reporting, literature, politics, and in education. For most everyday conversation, Arabic-speaking countries tend not to use MSA but instead use their own spoken dialects that vary country to country, and even region to region. The varieties of Arabic spoken in Saudi Arabia include Najdi Arabic, Hijazi Arabic, and Gulf Arabic.

Arabic is known for its unique and ornate script, which is written from right to left. There are twenty-eight letters in the Arabic alphabet, and each letter has three forms depending on whether it falls at the beginning, middle, or end of a word. Vowel sounds are indicated by markings above and below words, which are omitted in everyday writing. Arabic is a complex language, but far from impossible to learn. The grammar can be challenging to some, but your vocabulary will grow quickly due to the system of trilateral root words. By adding to the root words or modifying them according to the structure of Arabic grammar, you can easily form a vast number of new words.

Although learning Arabic will enrich your time in the Kingdom and afford tangible advantages, it is not strictly necessary for the purposes of working here. Many Saudis speak English fluently, often because they have lived or been educated abroad, though their written English may not be at the same level. Some young people even speak better English than Arabic nowadays, thanks to social media, free resources online, and watching English movies growing up—and they love to speak English with foreigners when possible. French is also sometimes spoken among the upper classes, especially the older generation.

Learning Arabic

Foreigners who make the effort to learn Arabic find that it opens a new world for them, both in practical understanding and in good will from their hosts—the Saudis are often deeply grateful to those who make the effort to understand their culture. Ambitious expats who want to take the plunge and bridge the linguistic divide will find the following resources helpful:

- Arabicpod101.com
- Arabius.com
- Italki.com

COMMUNICATION STYLE

Saudi Arabia is a classic example of a high-context culture. The terms "high context" and "low context" were coined by the interculturalist Edward Hall and describe two broad categories of behaviors that characterize how cultures communicate, develop relationships, work together, and utilize time. Being aware of and familiar with the two different communication styles will allow you to communicate more effectively.

High-context communicators tend to speak indirectly, generally avoid conflict, and try to maintain harmony in working groups. The indirect communication style is often incorrectly interpreted as "avoiding the truth" or "hiding something"—on the contrary, the objective is more to preserve the relationship and prevent people (yourself as well as others) from unnecessary embarrassment. It's not uncommon to hear Western expats say something like: "I don't know what they are really thinking!" or "He didn't tell me much detail!" It's important to realize that it's an implicit style of communication, that the meaning sometimes has to be worked out according to the context, and that learning to do so can take some time. Equally important is to understand that there is no ill intent when it seems that someone may be avoiding or speaking around an issue, and that it goes hand in hand with the relationship orientation of these cultures.

In general, high-context communicators usually prefer verbal, face-to-face communication and don't place much emphasis on written communication. This is also true for working in Saudi: it's always more effective to discuss things with people in person. Emails can be vague, depending on

the level of written English of the people you are writing
to, and written communications can go unanswered.
Other cultures which are on the high-context end of the
spectrum are India, Brazil, Thailand, Greece, Turkey, Iran,
China, Japan, Korea, and Vietnam.

Low-context culture and communication style is the
norm in the United States, Canada, the UK, Ireland,
Australia, and New Zealand, to varying degrees. These
cultures tend to be more task-oriented than relationship-
oriented. They often place a large emphasis on written
communication, and tend to write in structured messages.
Communication tends to be more direct, precise, and
to the point. Clarity is important, and so are agendas,
schedules, punctuality, organization, and planning.

ETIQUETTE AND BODY LANGUAGE

Generally speaking, physical contact or public displays of
affection between genders is not considered acceptable,
although married couples holding hands in public is
permissible. If you find yourself in a new situation, it's
always advisable to wait and see what the opposite-gender
Saudi does; if they extend their hand to shake yours,
it's okay to shake it. As Saudi continues to modernize,
more people take on the Western habit of shaking hands,
particularly younger Saudis. Those who decline do so for
reasons of modesty and will place a hand over their heart
in a gesture of sincerity.

You may find that some Saudis tend to be restless,
fiddling with their prayer beads, shifting in their chairs,

or checking their phones often. This doesn't mean that they are bored with your conversation; it may well be that they've had too much caffeine. Foreign teachers who work in Saudi sometimes find difficulty in getting students to sit still—all ages up to and including adults.

Saudis may glance quizzically at foreigners, but they rarely stare, meaning that women visitors from abroad will feel more comfortable here than many other countries. To avoid looking at women's bodies or acting indecently toward them is a cultural value with its root in Islam. One such verse from the Qur'an reads: "Tell believing men to lower their gaze and guard their modesty. That will be purer for them. For Allah is aware of what they do." [24:30] In fact, the politest way for a man to treat a woman he doesn't know is to ignore her. Male friends hug and kiss each other on the cheek when they meet. Women will also kiss each other on alternating cheeks—sometimes seven times!

To express respect, a person might remain standing in the presence of seated elders, or sit upright on the edge of their chairs. It would be rude to slump in your chair when sitting with someone of greater age. Among equals and long-term familiars, it's acceptable to lounge comfortably, even sprawl across the comfortable red cushions commonly used in hosting rooms.

It's rude to point the soles of your feet at someone you are with, because they are in contact with the unclean ground (by extension, slapping someone with a shoe is an expression of utter contempt), but that doesn't apply to people at the next table in a café, for example, who are outside the social circle.

In public and in workplaces, if a man is waiting for an elevator with a woman he doesn't know, he will let her go up in the elevator first, on her own, and will wait for the next elevator.

A Point of Pride

In one incident, an expat arrived at work to find that someone from his team had parked within the team's designated area, but in a no-parking spot. Assuming it was an honest error, and not knowing exactly whose car it was, the expat sent a message to the team's WhatsApp group to alert the person of the misdirected parking. The expat thought he was doing the person a favor as the car may have received a parking ticket with a fine. Later that day, he found one of his Saudi teammates was not speaking to him; it was his car parked in the no-parking spot. Evidently his teammate had been embarrassed by the group message with the photo of his car parked in the wrong place and it took a few months to repair the relationship.

In analyzing the situation, the expat asked a Saudi friend how he should have handled it, and the Saudi friend told him that he shouldn't have sent any message. "So you would let the person get a parking ticket?" he asked, incredulously. "Yes—that's *his* problem. It's worse to publicly embarrass him in front of his colleagues, though."

Other ways to show good manners are to demonstrate patience, flexibility, and gratitude for your Saudi friends and colleagues' efforts and kindness. Try to keep your behavior and conduct on an even keel at all times.

The most important thing to remember is that, being a guest in a foreign country, you need to adjust to their ways, and not the other way around. Some adamant expats get upset, storm into offices and proclaim, "This is not the way it's done!" without realizing that he has brought his own perception of "the way it's done" from his home country—which doesn't necessarily apply here. Respecting the hierarchy of the place or organization will only work in your favor.

PHONES AND SIM CARDS

As in most countries around the world today, landline telephones are seldom used anymore except in offices. The most popular companies for reliable cell phone packages are Mobily, STC, and Zain. Be sure to get one with a good internet allowance and an international calling plan if you want to make frequent calls back home. You can also use internet apps, though not all of them will work for making calls. WhatsApp calling, for example, doesn't work in Saudi. You can currently use Facebook Messenger, Duo, Telegram, Snapchat, Facetime, and sometimes Botim for internet-based calls from your cell phone, however.

SIM cards can be purchased in many locations, from the airport to retail stores. It's advisable to buy one in the airport upon arrival, since you need internet for almost everything—from calling a taxi to ordering food. Subsequently you can "recharge" via the phone company's app if you run out of data or credit. You need to show your passport and visa to purchase a SIM card (any type of visa will do).

EMERGENCY PHONE NUMBERS

In the big cities, dial 911 for all emergencies.

In the smaller towns and rural areas, use 911 or the following numbers:

Ambulance 997

Fire 998

Police 999

Traffic Accidents 993

THE MEDIA

Newspapers

The most-read Arabic language newspapers are Saudi-based *Al Arabiyya*, *Okaz*, and for economic news, *Etqesadia*. There are several English language news options, which are mostly read online. The most popular ones include *Arab News* and the *Saudi Gazette*. Virtually all Saudi media and social networks could be subject to censorship at any time, so it's important to be mindful of posting or publishing anything that reaches the public eye.

TV and Radio

One of the most popular Arabic entertainment portals is MBC.net, which provides access to a mix of sports, series, movies, and music content. Japanese anime is popular and watched by many young Saudis. You won't find much Netflix binge-watching in Saudi, though—it is available, but as the Saudi government is not able to censor it, Saudis prefer not to watch it due to the fact that most programs contain issues which go against Saudi culture.

Although many people still listen to the radio while driving in their cars, podcasts are becoming more popular, particularly among younger Saudi listeners.

INTERNET AND SOCIAL MEDIA

Saudi Arabia is a highly connected society, where people spend on average of seven to eight hours per day online. Around three hours of that time is spent on social media.

In 2024 there were more than 36.3 million internet users, which accounts for nearly the entire population. The majority of connections are made via mobile phones, since almost all Saudis have a cell phone (and sometimes two); only 57 percent own a computer.

At one time in the not-too-distant past, many apps used around the world were banned in Saudi Arabia. Today, a wider range of apps are accessible, though websites that contain content deemed immoral or that violates the country's values or beliefs are blocked.

So which social media apps are most popular in the Kingdom? Of the 29 million active social media users, the most popular platforms are Instagram, TikTok, Snapchat, Twitter, YouTube, LinkedIn, Telegram, and Facebook. The app that wins the top position, however, is WhatsApp. Interestingly, 65 percent of social media users in the Kingdom are men.

No matter which platforms you're using, it's important to be attuned to local sensitivities when engaging with audiences online. That means, for example, not posting any sexually suggestive content or content that could be perceived as politically or religiously controversial. Digital platforms are monitored and there may be legal ramifications imposed if someone is caught posting such content.

Following global trends, online shopping has become increasingly popular in recent years, with Amazon, Noon, and Desertcart being the most widely used digital shopping platforms in the Kingdom.

MAIL

Saudi postal services are reliable, at least as far as sending things abroad is concerned. Letters from other countries usually arrive within a week. One problem is the absence of proper addresses: few houses have numbers and so many can only be described as "the third house behind the mosque on the left." As such, it's best to use your office address unless you live in a well-known compound. All major courier companies operate in Saudi these days, including DHL, UPS, and FedEx.

Ensure that packages arriving from abroad don't contain content or goods that violate Saudi cultural norms; incoming packages are inspected and if found to be offensive, are censored or confiscated by the authorities.

CONCLUSION

Saudi Arabia is an enigmatic country and one that is undergoing rapid transformation. What used to be a closed, secretive, and utterly conservative nation is now opening its doors, its hearts, and its businesses to people from the outside. While at one time, foreigners who spent time here felt they'd submitted to a life somewhat lacking in the comfort and entertainment options that they were used to back home, today both visitors and expats can experience a very full life in the Kingdom.

Beyond the beauty of the Red Sea, the serenity of the desert, the traditional architecture, and the varied landscapes, it's the Saudis themselves who make being in the Kingdom so worthwhile. Their charm, humility, generosity, and warmth mean that those who do visit often find themselves returning, time and again. By taking the time to learn about Saudi culture, values, and traditions you will find that your welcome is warmer still.

USEFUL APPS

Communication and Socializing

Stay connected with an eSim from **Airalo**. Get up to date on current events with **Arab News**. Meet new people via **Internations**, **Expatriate**, **Ravl**, **Meetup**, and **Eventbrite**. Brush up on your Arabic with **NEMO Arabic**, **Italki**, **Arabius**, and **Arabicpod101**.

Travel and Transportation

Hail a ride with **Uber**, **Careem**, **Bolt**, **Ego**, or **Jeeny**. Navigate using **Waze**. Plan rail trips using **Journey Planner / Map -Transit** and bus trips in Mecca with **Makkah Bus.** Book accomodation with **Booking** and **Airbnb**

Food and Shopping

For shopping online, use **Noon**, **Amazon.sa**, **Jarir**, **Tamara**. Meals and groceries can be ordered to your home using **The Chefz**, **Toyou**, **Jahez**, **Nana**, **Hunger Station**, **Talabat**, **InstaShop**, **Ninja**, and **Mrsool**. Supermarket delivery platforms include **Carrefour**, **Lulu**, **Danube**, **Tamimi**, **Clicflyer.** Medical and health items can be ordered from online pharmacy **Nahdi.** Send packages using **Spl Online.** Make digital payments locally using **STC pay**, **Moyasar**, **Payfort**, **Paytabs**, **and Hyperpay**.

PICTURE CREDITS

Cover image: *Traditional Arabic coffee pot or Dallah, served with saudi sweet dates.* © hussein farar/Shutterstock

Shutterstock: 12 by Hyserb; 15 by Galih ajasih; 17, 140 by AFZAL KHAN MAHEEN; 18 by Sergey_Bogomyako; 31 by murathakanart; 33 by Zoomworld88; 35 by choi yurim; 39 by Logen Wang; 42 by Emily Marie Wilson; 44 by HAFIZULLAHYATIM; 47 by Mohamed Reedi; 59 by Brilliant-Tariq Al Nahdi; 76 by badr_a_alfarsi; 78 by PIXELGRAPH MEDIA LLP; 79 by dieddin; 83 by Sony Herdiana; 87 by Hany Musallam; 97 by MohammadAzeem; 104, 128 by Emily Marie Wilson; 116 by schusterbauer.com; 118 by Hussam Alduraywish; 119 by eyetravelphotos; 120 by abdul hafiz ab hamid; 123 by PeopleImages.com - Yuri A; 126 by Leo Morgan; 130 by Andrzej Lisowski Travel; 135 by The Road Provides; 138 by Hyserb; 145 by cristiano barni; 147 by Crystal Eye Studio; 151 by Altug Galip; 153 by Rahul D'silva; 155 by Sapsiwai; 156 by adel awad Abdallah; 158 by Nesru Markmedia; 160 by Ziyad alangri; 163 by ahmad. faizal; 169 by T L; 175 by abdallah darabseh; 181 by ZouZou; 185 by Magic Orb Studio.

Unsplash: 14 by NEOM; 50 by mohammad alashri;

Public Domain: 30, 37

INDEX